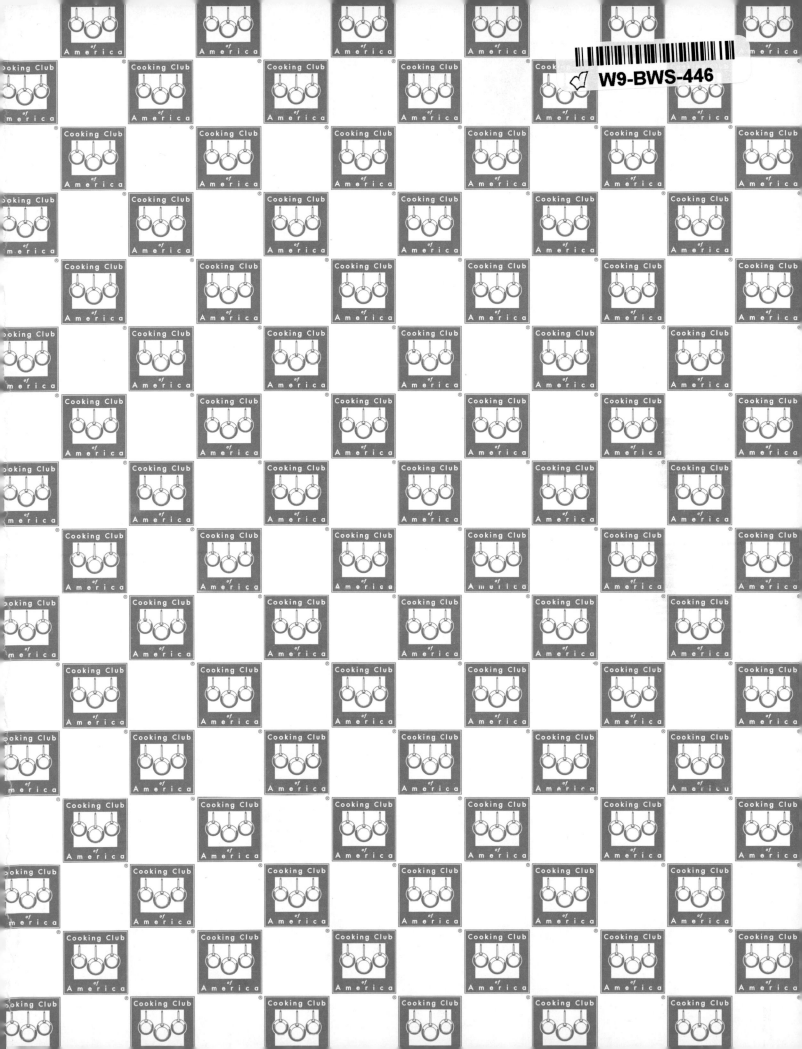

THE BEST OF
COOKING
PLEASURES

A Culinary Tour

Cooking Club
of
America ®

MINNETONKA, MINNESOTA

The Best of Cooking Pleasures—A Culinary Tour

Tom Carpenter
Director of Book Development

Michele Teigen
Senior Book Development Coordinator

Greg Schwieters
Book Design

Shari Gross
Book Production

Laura Belpedio
Book Development Assistant

Stafford Photography
Photography

1 2 3 4 5 6 7 8 / 06 05 04 03 02

ISBN 1-58159-165-9

Cooking Club of America
12301 Whitewater Drive
Minnetonka, MN 55343
www.cookingclub.com

Contents

The Best of
Cooking Pleasures
A Culinary Tour

Come along on *A Culinary Tour* of tastes and traditions in this volume of *The Best of Cooking Pleasures*.

Cooking, like life, becomes a little boring if you never branch out to tackle new challenges.

Sure, tried-and-true recipes are heartwarming and wonderful, and they virtually guarantee success. There's nothing wrong with that. But a wide world of cooking adventure awaits—a world you're striving to explore through activities like your membership in the Cooking Club of America.

A great way to start any new exploration, or keep a search going, is with a tour. Guided by a trusted source, this tour can give you an idea of what's out there so you can get excited and make a plan before diving in.

That's just what we created for you in **The Best of Cooking Pleasures—A Culinary Tour**. Here, in one beautiful book, are almost all the great feature stories published in *Cooking Pleasures* magazine in 2001.

Members always ask us for a complete, handsome and convenient summary of the year's magazine coverage; sometimes it's hard to keep track of all that great content. What better way than with a book packed full of all the great recipes, gorgeous photos and insightful cooking ideas and instruction? We're happy to oblige, once again.

So come along on this very special tour of cooking tastes and traditions. To start, tour fine cooking traditions from around the globe in Worldly Creations. Dig up great side dishes in Essential Accents. Discover new tastes in Shining Stars—feature recipes you'll love having in your repertoire. Savor the desserts and treats presented in Sweet Highlights. And learn how to cook with five very interesting feature ingredients, in Complete Stories.

The nice thing about this culinary tour is that you'll have the contents—the ideas, the recipes, the instruction—right at your fingertips always, ready to take you back out on another cooking journey.

Fresh from the Islands, page 8.

Roasted Corn and Red Pepper Salad, page 32.

Personal Meat Loaves, page 54.

Warm Chocolate Truffle Tart, page 95.

Individual Buttermilk Clafoutis with Plums, page 116.

Roast Chicken with Baby Beets, Asparagus
and Potatoes, page 136.

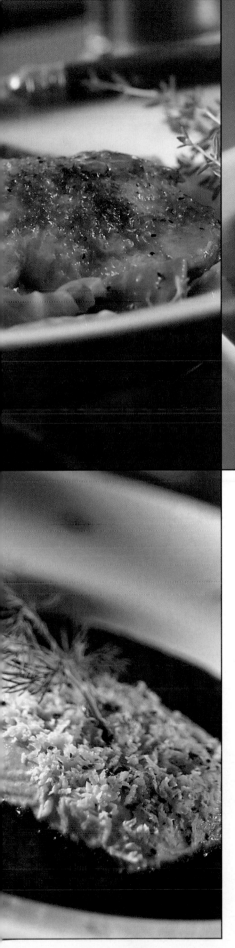

Worldly Creations

Recipes and menus from around the globe.

Fresh from the
Islands

Hawaiian Roast Pork with
Fresh Pineapple Salsa

A New Year's Day menu celebrates the flavors of Hawaii.

Text by Laurel Keser; Recipes by Monique Jamet Hooker

I grew up in Hawaii where New Year's Eve was celebrated with firecrackers that started in the afternoon and went off into the early morning hours. On the following day, neighborhood sidewalks would be littered with bits of red wrappers, reminding us of the previous night's festivities. We'd spend the day visiting friends, relaxing with family and enjoying a meal while we watched for whales and a beautiful sunset. I had those memories in mind when I created this Hawaiian menu for a New Year's Day gathering of friends. The menu is centered on island favorites: tempting fish appetizers, slow-roasted pork with an Asian-molasses rub, and chocolate cake triangles for dessert. While I can't guarantee you'll get a glimpse of whales or even a sunset, these island flavors may set the stage for a pleasant New Year's resolution: plans for a Hawaiian holiday.

Hawaiian Roast Pork with Fresh Pineapple Salsa

RUB
- 1 tablespoon salt
- 1½ teaspoons five-spice powder
- ½ teaspoon dry mustard
- ¼ teaspoon freshly ground pepper
- 2 tablespoons molasses

PORK
- 1 (4- to 5-lb.) boneless pork loin
- 1 tablespoon Dijon mustard

SALSA
- 3 cups chopped fresh pineapple (1 lb.)
- 2 or 3 jalapeño chiles, seeded, finely chopped
- 1 red bell pepper, finely chopped
- ½ cup finely chopped onion
- ⅓ cup chopped fresh cilantro
- ¼ cup lime juice
- ½ teaspoon salt

1 In small bowl, combine all rub ingredients; mix well. Rub over pork loin. Cover; refrigerate 30 minutes or overnight.

2 Heat oven to 425°F. Place rack in shallow roasting pan. Place pork on rack; add ½ inch water to pan. Bake, uncovered, 30 minutes or until browned.

3 Reduce oven temperature to 250°F; bake roast an additional 2 to 2½ hours or until internal temperature reaches 150°F, checking to make sure there is always some water in bottom of pan.

4 Meanwhile, in large bowl, combine all salsa ingredients; mix well. Cover and refrigerate.

5 Place roast on carving board. Cover loosely with foil; let stand 15 to 20 minutes. Whisk Dijon mustard into pan juices. Slice pork; place on serving platter. Pour mustard

Mauna Kea Chocolate Cake

sauce over slices. Serve hot or at room temperature with salsa.

12 servings.

PER SERVING: 290 calories, 12 g total fat (4 g saturated fat), 34 g protein, 9.5 g carbohydrate, 95 mg cholesterol, 755 mg sodium, 1 g fiber.

Mauna Kea Chocolate Cake

Coffee, chocolate and vanilla, all grown in Hawaii, are featured prominently in this cake, cut to resemble the mountains that dominate the landscape. The dessert can be baked a day or two ahead, then cut, glazed and refrigerated until ready to serve.

CAKE
½ cup strong coffee
3 oz. semisweet chocolate, chopped
¾ cup milk
½ teaspoon lemon juice or vinegar
½ cup unsalted butter, softened
1½ cups sugar
2 eggs
1 teaspoon baking soda
1 teaspoon vanilla
1½ cups all-purpose flour

SAUCE
2 egg yolks
3 tablespoons sugar
1 cup milk
½ teaspoon vanilla

GLAZE
6 oz. semisweet chocolate, chopped
3 tablespoons unsalted butter
3 tablespoons strong coffee
1 teaspoon corn syrup
1 teaspoon vanilla

1 Heat oven to 375°F. Spray 13x9-inch pan with nonstick cooking spray. Line bottom with parchment paper; spray and flour paper and pan. In small saucepan over medium heat, bring ½ cup coffee to just below a simmer. Remove from heat; add 3 oz. chocolate. Let stand until chocolate is melted; stir. Let stand until cool. In small bowl, combine milk and lemon juice; set aside.

2 In large bowl, beat ½ cup butter and 1½ cups sugar at medium speed until light and fluffy. Add eggs one at a time, beating until mixture is creamy. Beat in chocolate mixture and milk mixture. Stir in baking soda and 1 teaspoon vanilla.

3 Sift flour over batter; fold just until flour is blended. Pour into pan.

4 Bake 30 minutes or until toothpick inserted in center comes out clean. Cool in pan on wire rack 20 minutes. Run small knife around outside edge to loosen; invert cake onto wire rack. Cool completely. Remove parchment paper.

5 Meanwhile, in small saucepan, combine egg yolks and 3 table-spoons sugar. Stir in 1 cup milk. Cook over low heat just until mixture comes to a boil and coats back of spoon, stirring constantly. Immediately remove from heat. Stir in ½ teaspoon vanilla. Pour into medium bowl. Place plastic wrap directly on surface; refrigerate to cool.

6 Meanwhile, in medium saucepan, combine 6 oz. chocolate, 3 table-spoons butter, 3 tablespoons coffee and corn syrup. Heat over low heat until melted and smooth, stirring frequently. Stir in 1 teaspoon vanilla.

7 Place wire rack over baking sheet. Cut cooled cake in half lengthwise. Cut each strip crosswise into thirds. Cut each square diagonally (you will end up with 12 triangles). Remove

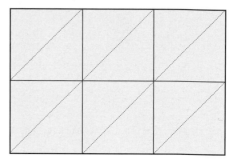

any loose crumbs; set each triangle, long side down, on wire rack. Spoon about 2 teaspoons glaze over each triangle, spreading glaze with small spatula. (Reserve remaining glaze to decorate plates.)

8 To serve, heat remaining glaze until warm. Place about 2 table-spoons vanilla sauce on each dessert plate, swirling gently to distribute sauce. Place cake in center of sauce on each plate. Spoon 3 large drops of glaze around front of each plate. Run toothpick or end of chopstick through each drop to form a sideways S, like a wave. For a tropical touch, garnish with an edible orchid or other edible blossom.

12 servings.

PER SERVING: 405 calories, 19.5 g total fat (11.5 g saturated fat), 5.5 g protein, 56 g carbohydrate, 100 mg cholesterol, 140 mg sodium, 1.5 g fiber.

Tiny Fish Cakes

Serve these cakes on a diagonal-cut slice of cucumber as an appetizer or on lightly sauced greens as a first course. If you can't find sweet chili sauce, hot pepper sauce and a spoonful of honey make a good substitute.

1	lb. tuna, mahimahi or salmon fillet
4	green onions, thinly sliced
½	red bell pepper, finely chopped
1	garlic clove, minced
2	tablespoons finely chopped fresh cilantro
1½	teaspoons Thai sweet chili sauce
1	teaspoon grated fresh ginger
½	teaspoon soy sauce
½	teaspoon salt
¼	teaspoon freshly ground pepper
1	egg
½	cup dry bread crumbs
2	tablespoons olive oil

1 Place tuna in food processor in small batches; pulse until finely chopped. Place in large bowl.

2 Add green onions, bell pepper, garlic, cilantro, chili sauce, ginger, soy sauce, salt, pepper and egg; mix well. Stir in bread crumbs. Refrigerate 30 minutes.

3 Shape into 24 small cakes, using about 1 tablespoon mixture for each; place on baking sheet. Cover tightly; refrigerate up to 1 day.

4 Just before serving, heat olive oil in large skillet over medium heat until hot. Add fish cakes in batches; sauté about 3 minutes or until lightly browned on each side, turning once. Serve hot.

12 (2-cake) servings.

PER CAKE: 50 calories, 2.5 g total fat (.5 g saturated fat), 5 g protein, 2 g carbohydrate, 15 mg cholesterol, 90 mg sodium, 0 g fiber.

Baked Bananas

Tropical cooks use plantains, or cooking bananas, for this dish, but any variety will do. Bananas should be on the firm and slightly green side rather than fully ripe.

2	tablespoons butter
3	tablespoons minced onion
6	large firm ripe bananas, sliced diagonally (½ inch)
3	tablespoons packed brown sugar
2	tablespoons fresh lemon juice
⅓	cup chopped macadamia nuts

1 Heat oven to 375°F. Melt butter in small skillet over medium heat. Add onion; sauté 2 to 3 minutes or until onion begins to soften, stirring occasionally.

2 Place bananas in 2-quart glass baking dish. Top with sautéed onions and butter. Sprinkle with brown sugar and lemon juice.

3 Bake 10 minutes. Stir; bake an additional 10 minutes or until bananas are soft. Sprinkle with macadamia nuts. Serve warm or at room temperature.

12 servings.

PER SERVING. 110 calories, 4.5 g total fat (1.5 g saturated fat), 1 g protein, 19.5 g carbohydrate, 5 mg cholesterol, 15 mg sodium, 2 g fiber.

Bowled Noodles

Buckwheat Noodle Soup with Fresh Spinach and Dill

Noodles carry the day in these Asian-inspired soups.

Recipes by Paulette Mitchell

As tradition goes, most noodle soups are heavy on the broth and light on the noodles. So what happens when you turn that tradition on its ear? Picture hearty noodles piled high in a deep bowl, splashed with a savory broth. Add a topping of crunchy vegetables and tender meat, and you're looking at a soup you can eat with a fork.

At the heart of these soups—and what makes them deliciously hearty—are Asian noodles. There are many varieties, each with a unique flavor and texture. They pair naturally with Asian flavorings, and the noodles we've chosen should be available in most grocery stores.

So grab a fork, or chopsticks if you prefer, and don't forget a spoon. You'll want to eat every morsel and drop of these satisfying soups.

Buckwheat Noodle Soup with Fresh Spinach and Dill

Buckwheat noodles infuse this soup with a deep, earthy flavor, while fresh dill provides a bright counterpoint.

- 1 tablespoon vegetable oil
- ⅔ cup chopped onion
- 4 medium garlic cloves, minced
- 6 cups reduced sodium vegetable or chicken broth
- 6 cups coarsely chopped baby spinach
- 2 cups frozen corn
- 1 carrot, cut diagonally into thin slices
- 2 green onions, finely chopped
- 8 oz. buckwheat (soba) noodles
- 1 tablespoon chopped fresh dill
- 2 tablespoons dark (Asian) sesame oil
  Dash ground white pepper

1 Heat oil in large pot or Dutch oven over medium heat until hot. Add onion; cook 3 to 4 minutes or until onion begins to soften, stirring occasionally. Add garlic; continue cooking 1 minute. Add broth; bring to a boil over high heat.

2 Reduce heat to medium-high. Stir in spinach, corn, carrot and green onions. Add noodles; cover and cook 7 minutes or until noodles are al dente, stirring occasionally. Stir in dill, sesame oil and pepper.

3 To serve, use tongs to transfer noodles and vegetables to individual soup bowls. Ladle broth over noodles.

4 (2-cup) servings.

PER SERVING: 395 calories, 12 g total fat (1.5 g saturated fat), 15 g protein, 67 g carbohydrate, 0 mg cholesterol, 460 mg sodium, 8 g fiber.

Vegetable Miso Soup with Udon Noodles

Miso, a slightly sweet and salty fermented soybean paste, is at the heart of traditional Japanese cooking. The lighter colored varieties are used in delicate soups and sauces, while the darker colored versions appear in heavier dishes. You'll find miso in the refrigerated section of supermarkets or at Asian markets or health food stores.

Shiitake-Chicken Soup
with Ramen Noodles

Shiitake-Chicken Soup with Ramen Noodles

Shiitake mushrooms give this soup its distinctive personality. If you can't find fresh ones, substitute dried shiitakes. To reconstitute them before using, cover them with boiling water and soak for about 5 minutes or until softened. As with fresh shiitake mushrooms, the stems are tough and must be removed.

2   tablespoons vegetable oil
1   tablespoon minced garlic
2   teaspoons minced fresh ginger
½   cup finely chopped carrot
¼   cup finely chopped red
      bell pepper
2   cups sliced shiitake
      mushroom caps
6   cups reduced-sodium
      chicken broth
2   tablespoons soy sauce
4   green onions, chopped
⅛   teaspoon ground white
      pepper
8   oz. boneless skinless
      chicken breast halves,
      cut into thin strips
2   (3.5-oz.) pkg. ramen
      noodle soup mix (discard
      flavoring packets)
1   medium tomato, chopped

1 Heat oil in large pot or Dutch oven over medium-high heat until hot. Add garlic and ginger; cook 20 to 30 seconds or until fragrant. Add carrot and bell pepper; cook 1 minute. Add mushrooms; cook 1 to 2 minutes or until mushrooms begin to soften.

2 Stir in broth, soy sauce, green onions and pepper. Bring to a boil.

3 Add chicken, noodles and tomato. Cover; cook 3 to 4 minutes or until chicken is no longer pink in center and noodles are al dente, stirring occasionally with fork to separate noodles.

4 To serve, use tongs to transfer chicken, noodles and vegetables to individual soup bowls. Ladle broth over noodles.

4 (2-cup) servings.

PER SERVING: 330 calories, 10.5 g total fat (2 g saturated fat), 22.5 g protein, 34 g carbohydrate, 30 mg cholesterol, 1280 mg sodium, 2 g fiber.

---

6   cups reduced-sodium
      vegetable or chicken broth
¼   cup light-colored miso
      (such as barley miso)
1   tablespoon vegetable oil
1   teaspoon minced ginger
2   medium garlic cloves,
      minced
8   oz. thin udon noodles
3   cups chopped bok choy
1   cup broccoli florets
½   cup thinly sliced baby
      carrots
½   cup frozen baby peas
2   teaspoons Asian chile-garlic
      sauce
1   (12.3-oz.) pkg. silken extra-
      firm tofu, cut into ½-inch
      cubes, room temperature
2   teaspoons toasted sesame
      seeds*
2   green onions, coarsely
      chopped

1 In food processor or blender, puree 1 cup of the broth and the miso.

2 Heat oil in large pot or Dutch oven over medium heat until hot. Add ginger and garlic; cook 30 to 60 seconds or until garlic begins to soften. Add miso mixture and remaining 5 cups broth. Bring to a boil over medium-high heat.

3 Stir in noodles, bok choy, broccoli, carrots, peas and chile-garlic sauce. Cover; cook 5 minutes or until noodles are al dente, stirring occasionally. Gently stir in tofu.

4 To serve, use tongs to transfer noodles and vegetables to individual soup bowls. Ladle broth over noodles. Garnish with sesame seeds and green onions.

TIP *To toast sesame seeds, heat small skillet over medium heat. Add sesame seeds; shake skillet continuously until seeds are lightly browned, 3 to 4 minutes.

4 (2¼-cup) servings.

PER SERVING: 480 calories, 15 g total fat (2 g saturated fat), 27 g protein, 64 g carbohydrate, 0 mg cholesterol, 780 mg sodium, 8 g fiber.

Shrimp Lo Mein Soup with Red Bell Pepper Salsa

Serve the salsa at room temperature, not chilled, so it will not cool down the hot soup. As you cook the soup, follow the timing carefully so the shrimp, noodles and asparagus are done at the same time.

SALSA
- 2 tablespoons fresh lime juice
- 1 jalapeño chile, seeded, minced
- 1 large garlic clove, minced
- 1 avocado, chopped
- ½ red bell pepper, chopped
- 1 green onion, chopped

SOUP
- 6 cups reduced-sodium chicken broth
- 2 tablespoons low-sodium soy sauce
- 2 tablespoons oyster sauce
- 8 oz. lo mein noodles
- 8 asparagus spears, cut into 2-inch pieces
- 1 lb. shelled, deveined uncooked medium shrimp
- 1 cup fresh bean sprouts

1 In medium bowl, stir together lime juice, chile and garlic. Add all remaining salsa ingredients; stir gently to combine.

2 Bring broth to a boil in large pot or Dutch oven over medium-high heat. Stir in soy sauce and oyster sauce. Add noodles and asparagus; cover and cook 3 minutes, stirring occasionally.

3 Stir in shrimp. Cover; cook an additional 1 minute or until noodles are al dente and shrimp turn pink. Stir in bean sprouts.

4 To serve, use tongs to transfer noodles, shrimp and vegetables to individual soup bowls. Ladle broth over noodles. Top each serving with salsa.

4 (about 2⅓-cup) servings.

PER SERVING: 490 calories, 12 g total fat (2 g saturated fat), 38 g protein, 58 g carbohydrate, 160 mg cholesterol, 1560 mg sodium, 6.5 g fiber.

Broiled Salmon with Asian Noodle Broth

When buying the salmon for this recipe, ask the seller to remove the skin. By broiling the salmon rather than cooking it in the broth, the fish browns and gets crispy edges, providing a visual and textural accent to the soup.

- 1 tablespoon vegetable oil
- 2 teaspoons minced ginger
- 4 garlic cloves, minced
- 6 cups reduced-sodium chicken broth
- 2 tablespoons low-sodium soy sauce
- 3 tablespoons hoisin sauce
- 8 oz. thin Asian noodles*
- 6 cups coarsely chopped baby spinach
- 3 cups sliced crimini mushrooms
- ½ cup coarsely chopped green onions
- 12 oz. salmon fillet (½ inch thick), skin removed, cut into 4 pieces
- 2 tablespoons chopped fresh cilantro

1 Heat broiler. Spray baking sheet or broiler pan with nonstick cooking spray.

2 Heat oil in large pot or Dutch oven over medium heat until hot. Add ginger and garlic; cook 20 to 30 seconds or until fragrant. Add broth; bring to a boil over high heat. Stir in soy sauce and 2 tablespoons of the hoisin sauce.

3 Reduce heat to medium-high. Stir in noodles, spinach, mushrooms and green onions. Cover; cook 3 to 4 minutes or until noodles are al dente, stirring occasionally with fork to separate noodles.

4 Meanwhile, brush salmon with remaining 1 tablespoon hoisin sauce; place on baking sheet. Broil 6 minutes or until lightly browned and fish just begins to flake, turning once.

5 To serve, use tongs to transfer noodles and vegetables to individual soup bowls. Ladle broth over noodles. Top with salmon; sprinkle with cilantro.

TIP *Use noodles made with wheat flour, not cellophane noodles or rice sticks.

4 servings.

PER SERVING: 410 calories, 12 g total fat (2 g saturated fat), 31 g protein, 44 g carbohydrate, 45 mg cholesterol, 1135 mg sodium, 4.5 g fiber.

Broiled Salmon with Asian Noodle Broth

Asian
Bounty

Vegetable-Tofu Skewers with
Soybeans and Rice

East meets West as Asian produce becomes a mainstay at farmers' markets across the United States.

Text and Recipes by Rosalind Creasy

We live in the golden era of produce. Farmers from New York to Los Angeles offer us the freshest herbs and vegetables. And today, with so many Asian enclaves in the United States, we have a treasure of Asian produce at our fingertips, particularly at farmers' markets. Chinese growers offer cabbages, greens and long beans; Japanese farmers sell eggplants, cucumbers and squashes; and Southeast Asians sell herbs, hot peppers and bitter eggplants. Years ago I was hesitant to buy this produce because it was unfamiliar, but I'm long over my reluctance. Asian farmers have shared their recipes with me and shown me how to use these ingredients in my own kitchen, from cooking fresh soybeans with rice to making Asian vegetable and noodle dishes.

Discover the fresh, crisp tastes of Asian vegetables. If you've hesitated buying them, let these recipes lead you into a world of new ingredients and flavors.

Vegetable-Tofu Skewers with Soybeans and Rice

Fresh soybeans are becoming more available, especially when sold under their Japanese name, edamame. If they are not available in your farmers' market, look in the frozen food section of a natural food store or Asian market, or substitute fresh peas.

MARINADE
- ⅓ cup soy sauce
- ¼ cup packed brown sugar
- ¼ cup dry sherry
- ¼ cup rice vinegar
- ¼ cup corn oil
- 4 teaspoons finely minced garlic
- 4 teaspoons grated fresh ginger
- 1 teaspoon hot sesame or chili oil
- 1 tablespoon sesame seeds

SKEWERS
- ¾ lb. Japanese eggplants (about 4 medium)
- 2 small yellow summer squash
- 2 small zucchini
- 1 large red bell pepper
- 1 (8-oz.) pkg. firm tofu

RICE
- 1½ cups short- or medium-grain white rice
- 1 cup fresh or frozen shelled soybeans
- 2 cups water

1 In large resealable plastic bag, combine all marinade ingredients; seal bag and shake to mix. Cut eggplants, summer squash, zucchini, bell pepper and tofu into 1-inch pieces; place in marinade. Seal bag. Refrigerate 1 to 3 hours, turning bag occasionally.

2 Heat grill. Meanwhile, rinse rice under running water until water runs clear. In medium saucepan, combine rice, soybeans and water. Cover; bring to a boil over medium heat. Reduce heat to low; simmer 15 minutes. Remove from heat. Let stand, covered, 15 minutes.

3 Meanwhile, thread vegetables and tofu onto 6 (14- to 16-inch) metal skewers. Reserve marinade.

4 When ready to grill, lightly brush grill rack with vegetable oil. Place skewers on gas grill over medium heat or on charcoal grill 4 to 6 inches from medium coals. Cook 8 to 12 minutes or until vegetables are crisp-tender, turning once.

5 Heat reserved marinade over medium-high heat 1 minute or until mixture comes to a boil. Serve vegetables with rice. Pass marinade separately; drizzle over rice or use as a dipping sauce.

6 servings.

PER SERVING: 435 calories, 11.5 g total fat (1.5 g saturated fat), 17 g protein, 67.5 g carbohydrate, 0 mg cholesterol, 490 mg sodium, 6.5 g fiber.

Asian Shredded Salad

Asian Shredded Salad

This variation on coleslaw combines many of the flavors of Southeast Asia. It's possible to substitute standard cabbage and chard leaves for the Asian greens. Make the salad a few hours before serving it so the flavors blend.

DRESSING
¾ cup mayonnaise
2 tablespoons rice vinegar
2 teaspoons minced fresh ginger
1 teaspoon hot pepper sauce
¼ teaspoon salt

SALAD
8 cups thinly sliced Chinese (napa) cabbage
2½ cups thinly sliced baby bok choy
1 cup chopped fresh cilantro
1 cup chopped green onions
½ cup chopped Thai basil, plus sprigs for garnish
2 tablespoons minced crystallized ginger
½ cup dry-roasted peanuts or cashews

1 In small bowl, whisk together all dressing ingredients.

2 In large bowl, combine all salad ingredients except peanuts. Pour dressing over salad; toss. Refrigerate 2 to 3 hours. Sprinkle peanuts over salad. Garnish with basil sprigs.

16 (½-cup) servings.

PER SERVING: 115 calories, 10.5 g total fat (1.5 g saturated fat), 2 g protein, 4 g carbohydrate, 5 mg cholesterol, 155 mg sodium, 1 g fiber.

Japanese-Style Noodles with Chicken

While we associate Asia mostly with rice, noodle dishes are also very popular. This variation on classic ramen noodle dishes is made with chicken; you can also make it with pork or shrimp, and thinly sliced daikon or pickled mustard cabbage can be added. Japanese, or Asian, noodles are vacuum-packed in plastic and are available in the refrigerated section in most Asian grocery stores and, increasingly, in standard markets as

well. (If fresh Japanese noodles are not available, dried Asian wheat or the wheat and buckwheat soba noodles can be substituted. Cook them according to the package directions until they are barely tender, and rinse them in cold water to stop the cooking process.)

1 (8-oz.) pkg. fresh Asian noodles*
2 tablespoons corn oil
2 boneless skinless chicken breast halves, cut into thin strips
7 cups sliced bok choy or mustard greens, separating stems and leaves
1 medium carrot, thinly sliced
1 small onion, finely chopped
½ cup reduced-sodium chicken broth
1 tablespoon minced fresh ginger
1 tablespoon Worcestershire sauce
1 teaspoon salt
½ teaspoon sugar
½ teaspoon chili powder or chili oil
1 green onion, sliced

1 Cook noodles according to package directions. Rinse with cold water; drain well.

2 Heat 1 tablespoon of the oil in wok over high heat until hot. Add chicken; stir-fry 3 minutes or until no longer pink in center. Remove chicken from wok.

3 Add remaining 1 tablespoon oil to wok; heat over high heat. Add bok choy stems and carrot; stir-fry 2 minutes. Add onion and bok choy leaves; stir-fry an additional 1 minute.

4 Stir in cooked noodles and chicken. Add broth, ginger, Worcestershire sauce, salt, sugar and chili powder; cook 1 minute or until hot. Garnish with green onion.

TIP *Fresh Asian noodles can be found in the refrigerator case of the produce section or in Asian markets.

4 servings.

PER SERVING: 375 calories, 10.5 g total fat (1.5 g saturated fat), 23 g protein, 48 g carbohydrate, 35 mg cholesterol, 1010 mg sodium, 4 g fiber.

Twice-Cooked Yard-Long Beans with Pork

This variation on a classic Chinese dish can be made as spicy as you like. Just increase or decrease the amount of chiles.

SAUCE
- ½ cup reduced-sodium chicken broth
- 1 tablespoon oyster sauce
- 1 tablespoon rice vinegar
- 1 tablespoon tamari soy
- 2 teaspoons sugar

BEANS
- 2 tablespoons vegetable oil
- 1 lb. yard-long beans, cut into 2-inch pieces (6 cups)
- ¼ cup finely chopped onion
- 2 oz. ground pork or 2 tablespoons shredded dried pork, minced
- 1 tablespoon minced fresh ginger
- 2 medium garlic cloves, minced
- 1 to 2 fresh green Japanese or Thai peppers, minced
- 1 tablespoon water
- 1 teaspoon cornstarch

1 In small bowl, stir together all sauce ingredients.

2 Heat wok over high heat until hot. Add oil; heat until hot. Add beans; stir-fry 5 minutes or until crisp-tender. Remove from wok.

3 Add onion, ground pork, ginger, garlic and chiles; stir-fry until pork is no longer pink.

4 Stir in sauce; bring to a boil. Simmer about 1 minute. In small bowl, blend water and cornstarch; add to sauce. Bring to a boil. Cook 1 minute or until sauce thickens, stirring constantly.

5 Return beans to wok; stir-fry until thoroughly heated.

4 servings.

PER SERVING: 155 calories, 9 g total fat (2 g saturated fat), 5.5 g protein, 14 g carbohydrate, 10 mg cholesterol, 415 mg sodium, 4 g fiber.

Stir-Fried Scallops with Asian Greens

This luscious light dish should be served over rice. Offer it as one of many Chinese main dishes, complementing it with a spicy dish, a meaty dish and one that is slightly sweet. It is critical that the scallops be fresh and sweet, and not "fishy" smelling. Combine different greens to give a depth of flavor.

- 1 lb. fresh sea scallops, halved
- 1 tablespoon minced fresh ginger
- 1 tablespoon rice vinegar
- 1 teaspoon vegetable oil
- ½ red bell pepper, finely chopped
- 10 cups sliced greens, such as bok choy, Chinese mustard, amaranth, Japanese red mustard, flat cabbage and/or Chinese cabbage
- ½ cup thinly sliced green onions
- 1 teaspoon salt
- 1 teaspoon sugar
- 2 teaspoons sesame oil

1 In medium bowl, stir together scallops, ginger and rice vinegar. Let stand while cooking vegetables.

2 Heat vegetable oil in wok over high heat until hot. Add bell pepper; stir-fry 2 minutes. Remove from wok. Add greens; stir-fry 2 minutes or until wilted. Remove greens from wok.

3 Add scallops and green onions; stir-fry 1 minute. Return bell pepper and greens to wok. Stir in salt, sugar and sesame oil; stir-fry until thoroughly heated and scallops are opaque, about 2 minutes.

4 servings.

PER SERVING: 135 calories, 4.5 g total fat (.5 g saturated fat), 16 g protein, 9.5 g carbohydrate, 20 mg cholesterol, 855 mg sodium, 2.5 g fiber.

Stir-Fried Scallops with Asian Greens

Asian Vegetables

asian eggplant

asian mustard greens

bok choy

chinese cabbage

An enormous variety of Asian produce is offered in markets across the country. We've spotlighted some of the more common items you're likely to find. Produce from farmers' markets is the freshest and most flavorful, but if you don't have access to one, check your local grocery or Asian food store.

Amaranth This leafy green and red warm-weather plant has a mild flavor and is best cooked briefly to prevent it from becoming mushy. Add it to stir-fries along with pork and garlic, or add it at the last minute to your favorite Asian soup. It will turn the soup light pink. Avoid wilted bunches, and use it within a few days.

Asian eggplant There are many varieties of Asian eggplants, but most are long and cylindrical. They're available in many shades of purple and white and are generally milder and less bitter than their European cousins. Choose unblemished eggplants that are firm and shiny. Refrigerate them in a paper bag for up to four days. They do not need to be peeled. Chinese cooking methods for eggplants include braising, frying, and cooking and serving cold with a sesame sauce. In Japan they are used in tempura, baked and served with savory dipping sauces, and pickled. They also can be cooked in a manner similar to their European cousins, and they are especially good for grilling.

Asian mustard greens These pungent relatives of cabbage include mizuna, Japanese red mustard and many types of Chinese loose-leaf mustard greens. In China, mustard greens are cooked in stir-fries with pork, blanched and served with oyster or sweet-and-sour sauces, added to soups and even pickled. In Japan, they are added to soups, or braised and served with a savory sauce. Western cooks enjoy the immature form of mustard greens and add them to mixed green salads.

Bitter melon Bitter melons resemble their cousins, cucumbers, but they have a decidedly bitter flavor. While treasured in much of Asia for their flavor, bitter melons are an acquired taste for Americans. Select green or white shiny, young melons. Avoid yellow and orange ones—they are the most bitter. Remove the seeds and spongy tissue before cooking. To mitigate the bitterness, slice the melons and sprinkle them with salt before cooking. Let them sit for 30 minutes, and then dry them on paper towels. Bitter melons complement strong flavors such as beef, garlic and onions. They're used in stir-fries and soups, or stuffed.

Bok choy The large bok choys that look like chard are a mainstay in much of China. There is also a miniature light-green variety, called Shanghai bok choy. When choosing bok choy, avoid wilted or yellowing leaves. Store it for a few days in a plastic bag in the refrigerator. The most popular way to serve the large bok choy is to slice the leaves and quickly stir-fry them with meats and seasonings. They are also good braised and served with roast pork or a black bean sauce. Often the Shanghai types are braised whole and served on a platter with mushrooms and a flavorful sauce. American cooks enjoy bok choy in dishes calling for chard.

Chinese broccoli Not really a broccoli, this kale-like green has succulent sweet stems and buds. Select shoots that are not wilted, have tight buds and are a bright green color rather than yellow. For the best flavor, use the broccoli within a day or so of purchase. To prepare Chinese broccoli, remove any large, tough leaves and peel the stems as you would asparagus. Cut the stems into 3-inch pieces for cooking in stir-fries with mushrooms, pork or seafood, and in soups and noodle dishes.

Chinese cabbage Chinese cabbage can be barrel-shaped, such as napa cabbage; tall and lacy, such as

Michihili cabbage; or loose-headed and dark green. All are milder than Western cabbages, and they're sweet and crunchy. Look for tight heads and a fresh appearance. Store them in the refrigerator for up to three days. Use these cabbages as you would common round ones, or enjoy them in stir-fries with seafood or a black bean sauce, in pot stickers and in hearty soups. Most Asian cuisines also pickle these cabbages for dishes such as kimchee.

Chinese long beans These beans, also called yard-long and asparagus beans, can be dark or light green, or purple. Related to black-eyed peas, not string beans, they have a rich meaty bean flavor. Select fairly firm pods without mature beans inside. The most traditional way to use them is in stir-fries with pork and chiles, or in soups. But they can be substituted in most recipes calling for green beans.

Coriander/Cilantro Americans call the leafy tops of the coriander plant cilantro, but in Asia it is known as fresh or leaf coriander. Avoid buying limp and yellowish bunches. To store it, trim the stems and place the fresh coriander in a jar of water. Cover it with a plastic bag and store it in the refrigerator for several days. The strong flavor of fresh coriander fades quickly, especially when cooked, so it is most often used raw in salads and dipping sauces, stuffed in Vietnamese salad rolls, or used as a garnish sprinkled over stir-fries, curries, soups and pasta dishes.

Daikon Asian radishes, known as daikons, are white, green or red and are usually cylindrical. Their average size is 12 to 18 inches long. Select firm, shiny roots and store them in the refrigerator where they will stay fresh for weeks. Daikons are staples for winter soups made with pork or fish; they can be cut into matchsticks and added to stir-fries; grated and added to soy sauce for dipping tempura; and made into pickles in dishes such as the Korean kimchee.

Flat cabbage (tatsoi) These dark-green, flat rosettes with white ribs are the aristocrats of the cabbage family. Choose shiny, fresh-looking heads and store them in the refrigerator for up to a week. A type of bok choy, mature flat cabbages are 12 inches in diameter and have a strong flavor. In China, they are braised, used in stir-fries with ginger, and served in soups with pork. Western cooks often use the tender, spoon-shaped leaves of the immature plants in mixed green salads.

Thai basil Thai basil is one of the characteristic flavors of Southeast Asia. It is similar to standard basil, except it has purple-tinged leaves and an additional cinnamon flavor. When choosing a bunch, avoid wilted leaves. Once home, trim the stems, put them in water and place the container on a windowsill, where it will stay fresh for days. Do not refrigerate it. The flavors of Thai basil fade when cooked. Often it is combined with mint and fresh coriander. It's used raw in simple salads, Vietnamese salad rolls or added to soup or Thai curry just before serving.

Thai peppers These peppers, usually hotter than an American cayenne, are added to Szechuan-style stir-fries and soups, Indian and Thai curries, Korean kimchee, Thai satay and Vietnamese dipping sauces. They are added to a dish whole (and removed before serving), grated or chopped. Authentic Asian dishes often call for four or five hot peppers. The two varieties most readily available in farmers' markets are the small but deadly hot Thai Dragon and Thai Hot. These are primarily sold green, though occasionally red ones are available. Look for shiny peppers that have no bruises or wrinkles. Fresh peppers can be stored in the refrigerator for up to 10 days. Red ripe ones can easily be dried in a warm dry place and used months later in stir-fries and hot-and sour soup.

chinese long beans

coriander/cilantro

thai basil

thai peppers

Brewfest

Chicken Braised in
Belgian Ale with Cabbage

Belgium's hearty cuisine and native ales inspire an entertaining menu.

Text and Recipes by Jill Van Cleave

Beer is to Belgian food what wine is to French cuisine. Not only is it enjoyed as a beverage with meals, it's also an integral ingredient in a variety of dishes. The nation's first breweries were part of monastic communities where beer was produced based on ancient Egyptian processes. Even though brewing evolved into a national industry over the centuries, Belgian master brewers have remained faithful to artisanal formulas. Today there are approximately 110 Belgian breweries, and many of these beers are available in the United States.

This Belgian-inspired meal features several styles of beer. When planning a beer menu, use lighter beers with appetizers and starters; then progress to stronger, more complex-tasting ales with the main course. Finish with a distinctively flavored dark beer. To really appreciate the beers, and to fully enjoy the meal, serve the same beer for drinking that you use in cooking. Then raise your glass, lift your fork and savor the flavors of Belgium.

Chicken Braised in Belgian Ale with Cabbage

In Belgium, this dish would be served with a side of "root mash" made of potatoes, celery root and leeks, a perfect accompaniment to soak up the delicious sauce.

CHICKEN
- 1 tablespoon butter
- 1 tablespoon vegetable oil
- 1 (4- to 6-lb.) chicken, cut up
- 1 teaspoon salt
- ½ teaspoon freshly ground pepper
- 1 large onion, coarsely chopped
- 1 large carrot, coarsely chopped
- 1 large garlic clove, chopped
- 2 tablespoons all-purpose flour
- 1 (12-oz.) bottle Belgian ale or other full-bodied beer
- 1 cup reduced-sodium chicken broth
- 3 juniper berries, crushed, chopped*
- 2 thyme sprigs
- 1 bay leaf

CABBAGE
- 1 (2-lb.) head green cabbage, quartered, cored, sliced (½ inch)
- 1 tablespoon olive oil
- ½ teaspoon salt
- ¼ teaspoon freshly ground pepper

1 Heat butter and vegetable oil in large nonreactive Dutch oven or heavy pot over medium-high heat until butter is melted. Sprinkle chicken with 1 teaspoon salt and ½ teaspoon pepper. Add chicken in batches to Dutch oven; cook 10 minutes or until browned. Remove chicken and pour out all but 1 tablespoon drippings from Dutch oven.

2 Reduce heat to medium. Add onion, carrot and garlic to Dutch oven; cook and stir 5 minutes or until softened.

Sprinkle vegetables with flour; cook and stir an additional 1 minute.

3 Add beer and broth. Bring to a boil. Add juniper berries, thyme and bay leaf; return chicken to Dutch oven. Reduce heat to low; cover and simmer 40 minutes or until chicken is tender and no longer pink in center.

4 Meanwhile, blanch cabbage in large pot of boiling salted water 5 minutes or until crisp-tender. Drain; cool under cold running water.

5 Place chicken on platter. Remove and discard thyme and bay leaf from Dutch oven. Skim fat from liquid. Increase heat to medium-high; boil 10 minutes or until sauce thickens. Return chicken to Dutch oven; cook until chicken is hot.

6 Meanwhile, heat olive oil in large skillet over medium heat. Add cabbage, ½ teaspoon salt and ¼ teaspoon pepper; cook 5 minutes or until hot. Spoon cabbage onto serving plates. Top with chicken and sauce.

TIP *Juniper berries, sold dried in the spice section, can be crushed by pressing them firmly with the side of a chef's knife.

6 servings.

PER SERVING: 405 calories, 20.5 g total fat (5.5 g saturated fat), 39.5 g protein, 15.5 g carbohydrate, 115 mg cholesterol, 800 mg sodium, 4 g fiber.

Cream of Belgian Endive Soup

This earthy soup may convince you to use endive for more than salad. The use of ale brings out the pleasant side of endive's natural bitterness while diminishing its astringent quality.

- 1 lb. Belgian endive
    (5 to 6 heads), cored
- 3 tablespoons unsalted butter
- 2 medium leeks (white part
    only), cleaned, halved, sliced
- 1 medium onion, chopped
- 1 medium red potato, peeled,
    chopped
- 3 cups reduced-sodium
    chicken broth
- ¾ cup white or blonde Belgian
    ale or light-bodied beer
- ½ cup whipping cream
- ¾ teaspoon salt
- ¼ teaspoon freshly ground
    white pepper

1 Reserve the smallest endive or half of a large endive for garnish. Coarsely chop remaining endive.

2 Melt butter in large saucepan over medium heat. Add leeks, onion and chopped endives; cook 5 to 7 minutes or until softened but not brown, stirring frequently.

3 Stir in potato and broth. Bring to a boil. Reduce heat to low; cover and simmer 30 minutes or until vegetables are very tender. Stir in beer. Remove from heat; cool slightly.

4 Carefully puree soup in batches in blender or food processor. (Recipe can be made up to this point up to 1 day ahead. Cover and refrigerate.)

5 To serve, bring soup to a gentle boil over medium heat. Stir in cream, salt and pepper. Slice reserved endive into thin shreds. Ladle soup into bowls. Garnish with shredded endive.

6 servings.

PER SERVING: 180 calories, 13 g total fat (7.5 g saturated fat), 5 g protein, 12 g carbohydrate, 40 mg cholesterol, 560 mg sodium, 3 g fiber.

Melting Belgian Chocolate Cakes

Chocolate lovers will be delighted to discover oozing interiors when this intensely chocolate dessert is cut open. It is important to use the highest quality bittersweet chocolate, and few would argue against Belgian Callebaut as a first choice.

CAKES
- Unsweetened cocoa
- 6 oz. bittersweet chocolate,
    finely chopped
- ¾ cup unsalted butter, cut up
- 3 eggs
- 3 egg yolks
- ½ cup sugar
- 3 tablespoons Belgian dark
    ale or full-bodied beer
- ½ cup all-purpose flour

CREAM
- ¾ cup whipping cream
- 2 tablespoons superfine sugar
- ¼ teaspoon vanilla

1 Heat oven to 450°F. Butter 6 (6-oz.) custard cups. Lightly sprinkle unsweetened cocoa over interiors; shake out excess. Set cups on baking sheet.

2 In microwave-safe bowl, combine chocolate and butter. Microwave on medium 1 to 3 minutes or until almost melted. Stir until smooth.

3 With whisk, beat eggs, egg yolks, ½ cup sugar and beer in large bowl until well blended. Stir in chocolate mixture. Stir in flour until thoroughly blended. Divide mixture evenly into custard cups. (Filled cups can be held in refrigerator up to 2 hours before baking.)

4 In another large bowl, beat all cream ingredients at medium-high speed until stiff peaks form.

5 When ready to serve, bake cakes on baking sheet 12 to 13 minutes or until tops are dry and outside edges just begin to pull away from edge of cups. (Centers may be slightly sunken but will rise as they sit.) Place on wire rack; cover loosely with foil. Let stand 4 minutes. (Internal temperature should be 160°F.)

6 With hot pad or towel, hold each cup and run knife around edges to loosen cakes; unmold hot cakes onto serving plates. Serve immediately; pass whipped cream separately. Store in refrigerator.

6 servings.

PER SERVING: 615 calories, 46 g total fat (27 g saturated fat), 8 g protein, 48.5 g carbohydrate, 310 mg cholesterol, 50 mg sodium, 2 g fiber.

Melting Belgian Chocolate Cakes

Tequila!

Jalapeño-Tequila Marinated Shrimp

Put a little kick in your cooking with Mexico's much-loved spirit.

Text and Recipes by Steven Raichlen

Let the French have their cognac, the English, their gin; when it comes to spirits, I raise my glass for tequila. Born under a blazing sun in the parched hills of central Mexico, tequila is custom-made for satisfying summertime thirst. It's also an ingredient I like to use in cooking.

Tequila adds an earthy sweetness to dishes ranging from salsas and seafood to dessert. It's fine to cook with the less expensive tequilas, although, as with all spirits, don't use any tequila for cooking that you wouldn't willingly drink. For a fuller taste, use a tequila made from 100 percent blue agave. Whichever tequila you cook with, use it sparingly. What tastes great in a margarita can quickly become overpowering and bitter-tasting in a sauce or dessert.

Jalapeño-Tequila Marinated Shrimp

These shrimp take about 10 minutes of actual preparation time, but the flavor is so vibrant, people will think you've been cooking for hours. If you want a more fiery taste, don't remove the veins and seeds from the jalapeños.

SHRIMP
2¼ lbs. shelled, deveined uncooked jumbo shrimp

MARINADE
2 cups coarsely chopped loosely packed fresh cilantro
4 to 6 jalapeño chiles, veins and seeds removed, coarsely chopped
½ small onion, coarsely chopped
3 garlic cloves, coarsely chopped
¼ cup fresh orange juice
¼ cup fresh lime juice
¼ cup extra-virgin olive oil
2 tablespoons tequila
1 teaspoon salt
½ teaspoon each sugar, cumin and freshly ground pepper

GARLIC-CILANTRO BUTTER
6 tablespoons butter
2 garlic cloves, chopped
3 tablespoons chopped fresh cilantro

GARNISH
2 limes, cut into wedges

1 Thread shrimp onto 6 (10- to 12-inch) metal or bamboo skewers. (If using bamboo skewers, soak in water 20 minutes. Then insert 2 skewers into each shrimp; this keeps them from slipping.) Arrange kabobs in shallow baking dish.

2 In food processor, combine cilantro, chiles, onion and 3 garlic cloves; finely chop. Gradually add all remaining marinade ingredients, processing until bright-green paste forms. Pour mixture over shrimp. Cover; refrigerate 30 to 60 minutes, turning kabobs several times to marinate evenly.

3 Melt butter in small saucepan over medium heat. Add 2 garlic cloves and 3 tablespoons cilantro; cook 2 minutes or until garlic just begins to soften, stirring occasionally.

4 When ready to serve, heat grill or broiler. Drain kabobs; discard marinade. Place kabobs on gas grill over medium heat or on charcoal grill 4 to 6 inches from medium coals, or broil 4 to 6 inches from heat 2 to 3 minutes on each side or until shrimp turn pink, basting with garlic-cilantro butter. Serve with lime wedges.

6 servings.

PER SERVING: 260 calories, 15 g total fat (8 g saturated fat), 26.5 g protein, 4 g carbohydrate, 275 mg cholesterol, 455 mg sodium, 1 g fiber.

Banana Sundaes with Mexican Chocolate Sauce

Bananas Foster meets chocolate fondue in this irresistible dessert. The dish is actually rooted in an ancient Mexican tradition—chocolate flavored with cinnamon, cloves and ground almonds. We call for apple bananas—small stubby bananas with a pleasing apple acidity, but small regular bananas can also be used.

CHOCOLATE SAUCE
- ¾ cup heavy whipping cream
- 6 oz. semisweet chocolate, coarsely chopped
- ½ teaspoon cinnamon
- ¼ teaspoon ground cloves
- 1 teaspoon vanilla

BANANAS
- 6 apple bananas or small regular bananas
- 3 tablespoons butter
- 3 tablespoons packed brown sugar
- 2 tablespoons rum
- 1 tablespoon tequila

ICE CREAM
- 3 cups vanilla ice cream
- ¼ cup slivered almonds, toasted

1 In heavy medium saucepan, combine cream, chocolate, cinnamon and cloves. Cook over low heat 6 minutes or until chocolate is melted, whisking occasionally until thick and smooth. Do not boil or chocolate may burn. Stir in vanilla. Remove from heat. (Chocolate sauce can be prepared up to 4 days ahead. Cover and refrigerate.)

2 Just before serving, cut bananas crosswise in half at a sharp diagonal. Melt butter in large nonstick skillet over medium heat. Increase heat to high; add bananas and brown sugar. Cook 2 minutes or until bananas are soft and a thick, syrupy sauce has formed, gently stirring occasionally. Add rum and tequila; boil 1 to 2 minutes or until slightly thickened.

3 To serve, scoop ice cream into 6 bowls. Spoon banana mixture over top. Drizzle with chocolate sauce. Sprinkle with almonds. Serve immediately.

6 servings.

PER SERVING: 555 calories, 34 g total fat (19.5 g saturated fat), 6 g protein, 63.5 g carbohydrate, 80 mg cholesterol, 110 mg sodium, 4.5 g fiber.

Banana Sundaes with Mexican Chocolate Sauce

Drunken Salsa

This salsa's handsome mahogany color, smoky flavor and gentle heat come from a long, wrinkled, brown or black dried pepper called chile pasilla. (Look for it in large supermarkets or Mexican markets.) The Mexican version of this salsa is flavored with a fermented drink called pulque; this one uses beer and tequila.

- ¼ cup vegetable oil
- 8 pasilla chiles (about 2 oz.)
- 1 large white onion, finely chopped (about 2 cups)
- ⅔ cup water
- ½ cup beer
- ½ cup distilled white vinegar
- 2 tablespoons tequila
- 1 teaspoon honey
- ¼ cup chopped fresh cilantro
- 1½ teaspoons salt
- ½ teaspoon freshly ground pepper
- ½ cup (2 oz.) crumbled salty cheese (such as Mexican queso fresco or feta)

1 Heat oil in medium skillet over medium heat until hot. Add chiles a few at a time; cook 10 to 20 seconds on each side or until puffed and crisp. Watch carefully; do not let them burn. Drain on paper towels; cool. Wearing gloves, remove stems from chiles; discard stems. Break chiles into 1-inch pieces. (Remove seeds and veins for a less spicy version.)

2 Add onion to skillet; cook 4 minutes or until golden brown, stirring frequently. Cool slightly.

3 Transfer onion and oil to food processor. Add chiles, water, beer, vinegar, tequila, honey, cilantro, salt and pepper; blend until coarse puree forms. Place in bowl; cover and refrigerate. (Salsa can be made up to 3 days ahead. Cover and refrigerate.)

4 Just before serving, sprinkle with cheese. Serve at room temperature with basket of chips for dipping.

3 cups.

PER 2 TABLESPOONS: 65 calories, 5 g total fat (1 g saturated fat), 1 g protein, 3.5 g carbohydrate, 0 mg cholesterol, 300 mg sodium, .5 g fiber.

Tequila with Sangrita

Sit down to any serious meal in Mexico and you'll be offered twin glasses of sipping tequila and sangrita. The latter is a spicy "chaser" based on tomato and orange or lime juice, often with a little chili powder or pickled pepper juice for punch. The presentation might be rounded out with a few radishes, scallions or jicama slices to munch on. Serve a fine sipping tequila, such as Don Julio, Perfidio or Patron.

- ¾ cup tomato juice
- ½ cup fresh orange juice
- 3 tablespoons fresh lime juice
- 1 tablespoon juice from pickled jalapeño chiles*
- 1 tablespoon finely grated onion with juice
- 2 lime wedges
- ¼ cup chili powder
- 1 bunch radishes, stems removed, radishes halved (about 1¼ cups)
- ½ small jicama, peeled, thinly sliced
- 9 oz. tequila

1 In pitcher, stir together tomato juice, orange juice, lime juice, chile juice and onion.

2 Moisten rims of 6 shot or cordial glasses with lime wedges. Place chili powder in shallow bowl. Invert glasses; dip in chili powder to coat rims.

3 Arrange radishes and jicama on platter. Pour sangrita into chili-dusted glasses. Serve tequila in separate glasses. Invite guests to sip tequila and sangrita alternately, eating radishes and jicama between sips.

TIP *Look for jalapeño chiles that are packed in vinegar.

6 servings.

PER SERVING: 145 calories, 1 g total fat (0 g saturated fat), 1.5 g protein, 10.5 g carbohydrate, 0 mg cholesterol, 170 mg sodium, 4 g fiber.

Tequila Basics

Tequila is a distilled spirit made from a sharp-leafed plant in the lily family called agave. The agave grows throughout Mexico. In Aztec times, the spiny plant was used to make the first alcoholic beverage in North America, a sort of wine the Aztecs called pulque.

The arrival of the Spanish brought a thirst for hard spirits and the technique of distillation. With brandy supplies running low, the Spanish filled their stills with pulque to make a potent spirit called mescal. Tequila is a special sort of mescal, the way cognac is a special sort of brandy. In time, connoisseurs observed that the best agave spirits came from a town in the dusty hills of central Mexico called Tequila.

Four factors distinguish tequila from ordinary mescal. First, it's made exclusively from the blue agave, one of 300 cactus species that grow in Mexico. Second, it only can be made from blue agave grown in a small, strictly delineated region north of Guadalajara in the state of Jalisco. Third, like cognac, it must be distilled not once, but twice, to remove undesirable flavors. And fourth, it must contain at least 51 percent distilled blue agave, the remainder being less expensive spirits or more agave.

There are four types of tequila. They differ depending on whether they're aged and for how long. To age tequila, it's placed in oak casks for several months to seven years. As with scotch, bourbon and cognac, barrel aging draws out harsh tannins, imparting an amber hue and subtle wood flavor.

Blanco (also called white, silver or platinum) is a clear, assertive, economical spirit that is bottled for immediate sale, without aging. It's best suited for mixed drinks.

Joven Abocado (also called gold) has been aged two to six months. It can be sipped straight (with salt and lime) or used for mixing.

Reposado is typically aged 8 to 10 months. This is often sipped straight up.

Añejo is the best tequila. It owes its finesse to a minimum aging of one year, with some aged up to seven years. As with the reposados, these are best enjoyed when sipped straight up.

Most tequilas are actually a blend of distilled agave and less expensive grain spirits (up to 49 percent of the latter). Premium tequilas are made from 100 percent agave, possessing a rich, full sweet flavor you can't beat.

Essential
Accents

Wonderful sides, finishing touches.

Roasted Corn and Red Pepper Salad

Capture the essence of seasonal produce in these simple dishes.

Text and Recipes by Georgeanne Brennan

Late summer in Provence, France, where I have a cooking school, means daily trips to the markets. I take my students early in the morning to find the best produce. This time of year, the season's vegetables reach their peak—and their fullest, purest flavors. So it's the best time to prepare simple side dishes that showcase the produce.

Of course, you don't have to be in France to enjoy such bounty. Local farmers' markets and grocery stores are packed with possibilities for sides that take little effort and use few ingredients. Make a tantalizing tart of lush, ripe tomatoes and creamy Gorgonzola cheese, a platter of vibrant green beans dressed with tapenade, or a colorful salad of roasted corn and sweet red peppers. When you have outstanding seasonal ingredients, focus on simplicity and the vegetables will shine.

Roasted Corn and Red Pepper Salad

Roasting the corn instead of boiling or steaming it gives it a nutty flavor that goes especially well with the sweetness of the peppers. Serve this to accompany barbecued steaks, ribs or chicken for a change from the usual corn on the cob.

- 8 ears corn, husks removed
- 1/3 cup extra-virgin olive oil
- 1 teaspoon salt
- 1 teaspoon freshly ground pepper
- 4 red bell peppers
- 2 tablespoons each chopped fresh oregano and parsley

1 Heat grill. Rub corn with about 1 tablespoon of the oil; sprinkle with 1/2 teaspoon each of the salt and pepper.
2 When ready to grill, place corn on gas grill over medium heat or on charcoal grill 4 to 6 inches from medium coals. Grill corn 10 to 15 minutes or until corn is slightly golden, turning occasionally. Meanwhile, add bell peppers to grill; cook 5 minutes or until skin is completely charred, turning occasionally.
3 Slice corn kernels from cob; place in large bowl. Remove skin, seeds and veins from bell peppers; cut bell peppers into 1-inch pieces. Add to corn. Toss with remaining oil, 1/2 teaspoon salt, 1/2 teaspoon pepper, oregano and parsley.
8 servings.

PER SERVING: 175 calories, 10 g total fat (1.5 g saturated fat), 3 g protein, 22 g carbohydrate, 0 mg cholesterol, 305 mg sodium, 3 g fiber.

Green Beans and Tapenade

The sweet nutty flavor of tender, young green beans is enhanced by tapenade, a Mediterranean olive spread. You can use more or fewer anchovies, according to your personal preference.

    1   cup pitted Kalamata olives
    3   tablespoons capers
    6   anchovy fillets
    2   garlic cloves
    ¼   teaspoon dried thyme
    3   tablespoons extra-virgin olive oil
    1¼ lbs. green beans

1 In food processor, puree all ingredients except beans to make a smooth paste.
2 Place beans in steamer basket over boiling water. Cover; steam 5 to 6 minutes or until tender. Drain; rinse with cold water to stop cooking.
3 To serve, place beans on platter. Spoon tapenade over beans.
4 servings.
PER SERVING: 180 calories, 14.5 g total fat (2 g saturated fat), 3.5 g protein, 11.5 g carbohydrate, 5 mg cholesterol, 610 mg sodium, 5 g fiber.

Fresh Tomato and Gorgonzola Tart

Sweet summertime tomatoes paired with creamy Gorgonzola make a delicious tart to serve warm for brunch, lunch or as part of a light supper.

    1   sheet frozen puff pastry
        (from 17.3-oz. pkg.)
    ¾   lb. plum tomatoes, thinly
        sliced (about 6 medium)
    1½ cups (6 oz.) crumbled
        Gorgonzola cheese
    ½   teaspoon freshly ground pepper
    ½   teaspoon minced fresh thyme

1 Place oven rack in bottom oven rack positon. Heat oven to 400°F. On lightly floured surface, roll puff pastry into 10-inch round, about ¼ inch thick. Place pastry in 9-inch tart pan; press in bottom and up sides. Press rolling pin over top to trim excess. With fork, prick bottom of crust all over.
2 Bake 10 minutes; remove from oven. If bottom of crust has puffed up, prick with knife in several places and it will slowly sink. Arrange about ⅔ of the sliced tomatoes evenly in bottom of crust. Sprinkle with cheese, pepper and thyme. Top with remaining ⅓ tomatoes.
3 Bake 25 to 30 minutes or until crust is golden brown. Place on wire rack; cool about 20 minutes before serving. Serve warm or at room temperature.
6 servings.
PER SERVING: 355 calories, 27.5 g total fat (12 g saturated fat), 8.5 g protein, 18 g carbohydrate, 30 mg cholesterol, 500 mg sodium, 1 g fiber.

Zucchini and Roquefort with Toasted Walnuts

Although quick and simple to make, this is a vegetable dish with character. It goes equally well with grilled hamburgers or more elegant fare, such as roast chicken or pork.

    3   small zucchini, thinly sliced
    3   tablespoons walnut or
        extra-virgin olive oil
    1   teaspoon red wine vinegar
    ½   teaspoon freshly ground
        pepper
    ½   cup (2 oz.) crumbled

Fresh Tomato and
Gorgonzola Tart

Roquefort cheese
¼ cup coarsely chopped
  toasted walnuts*

1 Place zucchini slices in steamer basket over boiling water. Cover and steam 3 minutes or until just tender.
2 In small bowl, whisk together oil, vinegar and pepper.
3 Place hot zucchini in serving bowl. Top with vinaigrette, cheese and half of the walnuts. Toss gently. Sprinkle with remaining walnuts.
TIP *Toast walnuts in dry medium skillet over medium to medium-low heat 3 to 4 minutes or until lightly toasted, stirring constantly.
4 servings.

PER SERVING: 210 calories, 20 g total fat (4.5 g saturated fat), 5.5 g protein, 4.5 g carbohydrate, 12.5 mg cholesterol, 240 mg sodium, 1.5 g fiber.

Roasted Beet Salad with Orange-Cumin Vinaigrette

Beets, among the sweetest of vegetables, lend themselves beautifully to salads. Here they're roasted for even more intense flavor, then dressed with a simple orange vinaigrette that's scented with cumin. You can roast the beets ahead if you like; refrigerate them until you're ready to assemble the salad. Trim the beet stem to 1 inch before roasting.

6 small beets
1½ teaspoons extra-virgin
   olive oil
2 cups young arugula leaves
   or watercress sprigs
1 tablespoon grated orange
   peel

VINAIGRETTE
1 tablespoon extra-virgin
   olive oil
2 tablespoons balsamic vinegar
2 tablespoons fresh orange juice
¼ teaspoon ground cumin
¼ teaspoon freshly ground pepper
⅛ teaspoon salt

1 Heat oven to 350°F. Rub beets with 1½ teaspoons oil; place in shallow baking dish.
2 Bake 40 to 50 minutes or until beets are tender and easily pierced with tip of knife. Cool slightly.
3 Meanwhile, in small bowl, whisk together all vinaigrette ingredients.
4 Peel beets; cut into ¼-inch slices. Place in medium bowl. Toss with 3 tablespoons of the vinaigrette.
5 Divide arugula evenly among 4 salad plates. Drizzle with remaining vinaigrette. Top with beets and orange peel.
4 servings.

PER SERVING: 100 calories, 4.5 g total fat (.5 g saturated fat), 2.5 g protein, 14.5 g carbohydrate, 0 mg cholesterol, 165 mg sodium, 2 g fiber.

Roasted Beet Salad with
Orange-Cumin Vinaigrette

Simple Toppings

Green Beans Top 1 lb. still-warm cooked green beans with mixture of 2 seeded chopped tomatoes, 1 tablespoon chopped fresh basil, ½ minced garlic clove, 1 tablespoon extra-virgin olive oil, ¼ teaspoon salt and ¼ teaspoon freshly ground pepper.

Zucchini Sauté 4 sliced small zucchini and 1 minced garlic clove in 1 tablespoon olive oil. Place in baking dish; top with ¼ cup toasted bread crumbs and ½ cup grated Gruyère cheese. Bake at 400°F. for 15 minutes.

Tomatoes Layer 4 thinly sliced tomatoes with 8 oz. thinly sliced fresh mozzarella cheese and 1 cup fresh basil leaves. Drizzle with mixture of 2 tablespoons orange juice, 1 tablespoon sherry vinegar, 1 tablespoon extra-virgin olive oil, 1½ teaspoons grated orange peel, ¼ teaspoon salt and ¼ teaspoon freshly ground pepper.

Sweet Peppers Toss 2 sliced roasted red bell peppers with ¼ cup chopped fresh parsley, ¼ cup halved pitted oil-cured black olives, 1 tablespoon extra-virgin olive oil and 1 teaspoon red wine vinegar.

Beets Top 4 sliced cooked beets with ½ cup crumbled blue cheese gently mixed with 3 tablespoons milk. Sprinkle with ¼ cup chopped toasted walnuts.

Leeks Top 4 sliced steamed leeks with 1 chopped hard-boiled egg, ¼ cup chopped fresh parsley, 1½ tablespoons extra-virgin olive oil, 2 teaspoons red wine vinegar, ⅛ teaspoon salt and ⅛ teaspoon freshly ground pepper.

Jams to Relish

Caramelized Onion-Garlic Jam

Beets, mushrooms and tomatoes take
center stage in these savory condiments.

Text and Recipes by Beatrice Ojakangas

Chutneys, ketchup and relishes, look out; there's a new kid in town, and it's got a savory reputation. Whether spread on bread or stuffed into mushrooms, "jams" made from vegetables add a low-fat flavor punch to whatever they touch.

By classic definition, jam is a thick mixture of fruit and sugar cooked until the fruit is soft and formless. Savory jams, on the other hand, are made with fresh vegetables, brightened up with herbs and spices. They're not sour, but they can be tangy—with the robust flavors of garlic, onions and even horseradish—and are cooked down to concentrate the flavors. Savory jams quickly jazz up sandwiches, grilled or roasted meats, poultry, fish and vegetables. Or they can be served at the table with other condiments.

Unlike homemade chutneys and ketchups, these savory jams are made with just a few ingredients that can be easily found, and they are quick to cook. The recipes that follow produce just a small amount to use within a few days. For longer storage, refrigerate the jams for up to two weeks or freeze them for up to two months.

Caramelized Onion-Garlic Jam

Don't skimp on the cooking time for the onions and garlic. The hour-long process allows the vegetables' natural sugars to caramelize, resulting in a wonderful deep, sweet flavor and golden color.

- 2 large sweet onions (about 1 lb.), coarsely chopped
- 1 bulb garlic, separated, cloves peeled, coarsely chopped
- ¼ cup extra-virgin olive oil
- 1 red bell pepper
- 1½ tablespoons chopped fresh rosemary or 1 tablespoon dried
- 1 teaspoon lemon juice
- ½ teaspoon salt
- ½ teaspoon freshly ground pepper

1 In heavy medium saucepan, combine onions, garlic and oil. Cover; cook over low heat 5 minutes. Remove cover; continue cooking 1 hour or until onions and garlic are very soft and golden brown, stirring occasionally.
2 Meanwhile, place bell pepper on grate over gas flame or directly on burner of electric stove. Cook over high heat until skin is completely blackened, turning pepper with tongs occasionally. Place pepper in heavy plastic bag; seal bag. Let stand 15 minutes or until cool enough to handle. Peel pepper under running water, removing charred skin. Slit pepper open; remove seeds and veins. Coarsely chop.
3 Place onion mixture in food processor; process just until coarsely chopped. Stir in bell pepper, rosemary, lemon juice, salt and pepper.

4 Cover and refrigerate. Serve at room temperature. (Jam can be made up to 2 weeks ahead. Cover and refrigerate.)
1½ cups.

PER 2 TABLESPOONS: 55 calories, 4.5 g total fat (.5 g saturated fat), .5 g protein, 3.5 g carbohydrate, 0 mg cholesterol, 100 mg sodium, .5 g fiber.

Spiced Tomato Jam

This sweet-and-sour spread is so tasty you'll be tempted to eat it straight out of the jar.

  6   whole allspice
  6   whole cloves
  ½   teaspoon crushed red pepper
  ¼   teaspoon mustard seeds
  1½ lbs. tomatoes (about 4 large)
  ½   cup sugar
  ½   cup cider vinegar
  ½   teaspoon salt
  ½   teaspoon freshly ground
       black pepper

1 On piece of cheesecloth, combine allspice, cloves, red pepper and mustard seeds. Tie with short piece of string, forming spice bag.
2 Bring large saucepan of water to a boil. Drop tomatoes into water; cook 1 minute. Remove from water. Peel tomatoes; cut into ½-inch pieces.
3 Place tomatoes and all remaining ingredients in heavy large saucepan. Add spice bag. Slowly bring mixture to a boil over medium heat. Reduce heat to low; simmer 1 to 1½ hours or until mixture is thick and most of the liquid has evaporated, stirring frequently. Remove from heat; remove spice bag with slotted spoon and discard.
4 Cover and refrigerate. Serve at room temperature. (Jam can be made up to 2 weeks ahead. Cover and refrigerate.)
1¼ cups.

PER 2 TABLESPOONS: 55 calories, 0 g total fat (0 g saturated fat), .5 g protein, 13.5 g carbohydrate, 0 mg cholesterol, 120 mg sodium, .5 g fiber.

Portobello Mushroom-Sage Jam

A bit of dark corn syrup brings out this jam's earthy mushroom and sage flavors.

  ¼   cup olive oil
  12 oz. portobello mushrooms,
       coarsely chopped
  ¾   cup finely chopped red onion
  1   garlic clove, chopped
  ¼   cup dry sherry
  ¼   cup chopped fresh sage
  1   teaspoon salt
  ¼   cup dark corn syrup

1 Heat oil in heavy large skillet over medium heat until hot. Stir in mushrooms, onion and garlic. Cook 2 minutes, stirring occasionally. Add sherry; simmer an additional 25 to 30 minutes or until mushrooms are very soft and liquid has evaporated.
2 Stir in sage and salt. Place mixture in food processor. Add corn syrup; process until mixture is coarsely chopped but not pureed.
3 Return mixture to skillet; cook an additional 5 minutes or until all liquid has evaporated.
4 Cover and refrigerate. Serve at room temperature. (Jam can be made ahead and refrigerated up to 1 week or frozen up to 2 months.)
1½ cups.

PER 2 TABLESPOONS: 75 calories, 4.5 g total fat (.5 g saturated fat), 1 g protein, 8 g carbohydrate, 0 mg cholesterol, 200 mg sodium, .5 g fiber.

Apple-Beet-Horseradish Jam

Tart and tangy, this attractive red jam goes well with roasted or smoked meats.

  3   small to medium beets
  3   tart medium apples, peeled,
       shredded (about 6 cups)
  ¼   cup sugar
  1   teaspoon caraway seeds
  ½   teaspoon freshly ground
       pepper
  ½   cup cider vinegar
  ½   cup finely grated fresh
       horseradish*

1 Place beets in medium saucepan; cover with water. Bring to a boil. Reduce heat; simmer 50 to 60 minutes or until tender. Drain; cool. Peel beets. With shredding disk on food processor, shred beets (there should be about 2 cups).
2 In large saucepan, stir together beets and apples. Add sugar, caraway seeds, pepper and vinegar. Bring to a gentle boil over medium heat; cook 12 to 15 minutes or until most of the liquid has evaporated, stirring occasionally.
3 place beet mixture in food processor; process until almost smooth but some texture remains. Stir in horseradish.
4 Cover and refrigerate until ready to use. Serve at room temperature. (Jam can be made ahead and refrigerated up to 2 weeks or frozen up to 2 months.)
TIP *¼ cup prepared horseradish can be used in place of the fresh horseradish.
2¼ cups.

PER 2 TABLESPOONS: 35 calories, 0 g total fat (0 g saturated fat), .5 g protein, 8.5 g carbohydrate, 0 mg cholesterol, 6 mg sodium, 1 g fiber.

Mushroom-Sage Crostini

Apple-Beet Reuben Sandwich

Spiced Tomato Jam with Grilled Chicken Breasts

Savory Serving Suggestions

You can use savory jams in many of the same ways you use marinades, salsas, chutneys and ketchup. Here are some suggestions to get you started.

Caramelized Onion-Garlic Jam

Shaved Turkey Sandwich with Caramelized Onion-Garlic Jam Toast sandwich bread; spread with mayonnaise and mustard. Layer with sliced tomatoes, shaved cooked turkey breast, Swiss cheese and Caramelized Onion-Garlic Jam.

Onion Jam Stuffed Mushroom Appetizers Fill large mushroom caps with Caramelized Onion-Garlic Jam; top with freshly shredded Parmesan cheese. Broil until cheese is melted and filling is bubbly.

Cream Cheese and Onion-Garlic Jam Crostini Slice loaf of French bread diagonally. Toast under broiler. Spread with cream cheese and Caramelized Onion-Garlic Jam. Garnish with fresh Italian parsley sprigs.

Roasted Vegetables with Caramelized Onion-Garlic Jam Roast variety of vegetables, such as eggplant, zucchini, bell peppers, potatoes and red onions. Toss hot vegetables with Caramelized Onion-Garlic Jam. Garnish with chopped fresh Italian parsley.

Portobello Mushroom-Sage Jam

Mushroom-Sage Crostini Slice loaf of French bread diagonally; brush with extra-virgin olive oil. Toast under broiler. Spread with Portobello Mushroom-Sage Jam. Top with halved cherry tomatoes and fresh sage leaves.

Tomato Salad with Mushroom Jam Arrange butter lettuce leaves on serving platter. Top with tomato slices. Spoon Portobello Mushroom-Sage Jam over tomatoes. Drizzle with olive oil and balsamic vinegar; sprinkle with salt and pepper. Garnish with fresh sage sprig.

Mushroom Jam-Smothered Steak Grill or broil your favorite steak until of desired doneness. Spoon Portobello Mushroom-Sage Jam over steak.

Pork and Portobello Jam Sandwich Spread slices of grilled Italian bread with Portobello Mushroom-Sage Jam. Top with thin slices of cooked smoked pork, tomatoes, sprouts and baby spinach.

Apple-Beet-Horseradish Jam

Apple-Beet Reuben Sandwich Spread 2 slices rye bread with mayonnaise and Apple-Beet-Horseradish Jam. Layer sandwich with shaved pastrami, sauerkraut and sliced Swiss cheese. Melt 1 tablespoon butter in heavy skillet; cook sandwich until golden on both sides. Serve with additional jam.

Potato and Apple Russian Salad Combine equal parts cooked diced potato and diced apple. Add enough thinly sliced green onion to provide color. Stir in enough mayonnaise and Apple-Beet-Horseradish Jam so that all ingredients are coated. Season with salt and pepper.

Rye and Apple-Beet-Horseradish Toasts Toast slices of rye bread. Spread with butter; top with thick layer of Apple-Beet-Horseradish Jam.

Spiced Tomato-Jam

Spiced Tomato Jam with Grilled Chicken Breasts Sprinkle skinless, boneless chicken breasts with salt and pepper; brush with olive oil. Grill or broil until chicken is no longer pink in center. While hot, brush with Spiced Tomato Jam; serve with additional jam.

Lamb Chops with Mint and Tomato Jam Brush lamb chops with olive oil. Grill or broil until of desired doneness. Brush both sides with Spiced Tomato Jam. Sprinkle with chopped fresh mint; serve with additional jam.

Tomato Jam and Brie Toasts Brush slices of French bread with olive oil. Broil until lightly toasted. Spread with soft brie; top with Spiced Tomato Jam.

Simply
Smashing

Mashed Sweet Potatoes with Caramelized Onion and Pancetta

The rustic texture of coarsely mashed root vegetables provides the foundation for the season's most comforting sides.

Recipes by Mary Evans

Root vegetables can take a beating and come out a winner. With a little mashing and some intriguing additions, they're easily transformed into fragrant, melt-in-your-mouth sides bursting with earthy goodness. Left rustically chunky, they're perfect accompaniments to autumn's hearty fare.

Because of their mild personality, root vegetables partner beautifully with assertive flavors. Carrots and ginger brighten parsnips' mellow nature for a dish that looks as good as it tastes. Potatoes and smoked cheese pair with rutabagas for a hearty-yet-fresh flavor. Sweet potatoes make a savory statement with the addition of caramelized onions and pancetta.

Whether you're serving a casual meal or a formal dinner, you'll want to save a place for these tasty clouds of culinary comfort.

Mashed Sweet Potatoes with Caramelized Onion and Pancetta

For a slightly firmer mixture, use a combination of sweet potatoes and russets. For the brightest color, choose orange sweet potatoes (sometimes labeled as yams), not white ones.

- 2 lbs. bright-orange sweet potatoes (about 3 medium), peeled, cut into 2-inch pieces
- 2 tablespoons olive oil
- 4 oz. pancetta, finely diced
- 1 medium onion, coarsely chopped
- 1 tablespoon red wine vinegar
- ¼ cup (2 oz.) mascarpone cheese or cream cheese
- ¾ teaspoon salt
- ¼ teaspoon freshly ground pepper

1 Boil sweet potatoes in large saucepan of boiling salted water over medium-high heat 15 to 20 minutes or until very tender. Drain sweet potatoes; return to saucepan.
2 Meanwhile, heat oil in large skillet over medium heat until hot. Add pancetta; cook 2 to 3 minutes or until beginning to brown. Add onion; cook 15 to 20 minutes or until onions are caramelized, stirring frequently. Adjust heat, if necessary, to prevent onions from browning too quickly. Add vinegar; stir, scraping up browned bits from bottom of skillet.
3 Over very low heat, mash sweet potatoes. Add mascarpone, salt and pepper. Stir in onion mixture.
8 (½-cup) servings.

PER SERVING: 245 calories, 18 g total fat (7 g saturated fat), 3 g protein, 18.5 g carbohydrate, 20 mg cholesterol, 310 mg sodium, 2.5 g fiber.

Carrot-Parsnip Smash

¾ lb. russet potatoes (about 2
    medium), peeled, cut into
    2-inch pieces
1¼ lbs. celery root (about 1
    medium), peeled, cut into
    1-inch pieces
1 medium onion, cut into
    2-inch pieces
1 tablespoon apple cider vinegar
1 tablespoon brandy, if desired
¼ cup sour cream
1 tablespoon chopped fresh dill
½ teaspoon salt
⅛ teaspoon freshly ground pepper

1 Place potatoes, celery root, onion
and vinegar in large saucepan. Add
enough water to cover. Bring to a
boil over medium-high heat. Reduce
heat to medium; boil 25 to 30 minutes or until very tender.
2 Drain vegetables; return to
saucepan. Stir in brandy. Over very
low heat, mash vegetables with
potato masher. (Vegetables should be
slightly chunky.) Stir in sour cream,
dill, salt and pepper.
6 (½-cup) servings.

PER SERVING: 90 calories, 2 g total fat (1 g saturated fat), 2 g
protein, 15 g carbohydrate, 5 mg cholesterol, 235 mg sodium,
3 g fiber.

Carrot-Parsnip Smash

*If parsnips are not on your regular
shopping list, they may be after you
taste this dish. Their pleasant sweetness beautifully complements the
other flavors.*

¾ lb. carrots (about 4), cut into
    1½-inch pieces
¾ lb. parsnips (about 3 medium),
    cut into 1½-inch pieces
1 medium tart apple, peeled,
    coarsely chopped
1 small onion, coarsely chopped
¼ cup crème fraîche or cream
    cheese
1½ teaspoons grated fresh ginger
¼ teaspoon salt
⅛ teaspoon freshly ground pepper

1 Cook carrots, parsnips, apple and
onion in large saucepan of boiling
salted water over medium-high heat
30 minutes or until very tender.
2 Drain; return to saucepan. Over
low heat, mash vegetables and apple
with potato masher. (Mixture should
be slightly chunky.) Stir in crème
fraîche, ginger, salt and pepper.
6 (½-cup) servings.

PER SERVING: 125 calories, 4 g total fat (2 g saturated fat), 1.5
g protein, 22 g carbohydrate, 10 mg cholesterol, 150 mg sodium, 4.5 g fiber.

Celery Root-Potato
Mash with Dill

*Celery root has a tendency to darken
when peeled. By adding a small
amount of vinegar to the water, the
celery root will retain its white interior.*

Celery Root-Potato Mash with Dill

Rutabaga-Potato Mash with Smoked Gouda

A wonderful, smoky cheese flavor permeates this chunky version of mashed potatoes. Delicious!

1¼ lbs. rutabaga (1 medium-large), peeled, cut into 1-inch pieces
1 lb. russet potatoes (2 medium-large), peeled, cut into 2-inch pieces
2 garlic cloves, peeled
1 tablespoon butter
½ cup sliced green onions
⅓ cup hot milk
1 cup (4 oz.) shredded smoked Gouda cheese
½ teaspoon dried thyme
½ teaspoon salt
¼ teaspoon freshly ground pepper

Rutabaga-Potato Mash with Smoked Gouda

1 Cook rutabaga, potatoes and garlic in large saucepan of boiling salted water over medium-high heat 25 to 30 minutes or until very tender.
2 Meanwhile, melt butter in small skillet over low heat. Add green onions; cook 3 to 4 minutes or until softened.
3 Drain vegetables; return to saucepan. Over very low heat, mash vegetables with potato masher, slowly adding milk during mashing. (Vegetables should be slightly chunky.) Stir in green onions, butter, cheese, thyme, salt and pepper.
6 (½-cup) servings.

PER SERVING: 185 calories, 7.5 g total fat (4.5 g saturated fat), 7.5 g protein, 22 g carbohydrate, 25 mg cholesterol, 415 mg sodium, 3 g fiber.

Butternut Squash and Potatoes with Parmesan and Rosemary

1 (14½-oz.) can reduced-sodium chicken broth
½ cup dry white wine
1 (1¾-lb.) butternut squash, peeled, cut into 1-inch pieces (about 5 cups)
1 lb. russet potatoes (about 2 medium), peeled, cut into 2 inch pieces
1 garlic clove, peeled
½ cup whole milk ricotta cheese
¾ teaspoon chopped fresh rosemary
¼ teaspoon salt
⅛ teaspoon freshly ground pepper
½ cup (2 oz.) freshly grated Parmesan cheese

1 Place chicken broth and wine in large saucepan. Add squash, potatoes and garlic; add enough water to cover vegetables. Bring to a boil over medium-high heat; reduce heat to medium. Boil 25 to 30 minutes or until potatoes and squash are very tender.
2 Drain vegetables; return to saucepan. Over very low heat, mash vegetables with potato masher. Stir in ricotta, rosemary, salt and pepper. Remove from heat; stir in Parmesan.
8 (½-cup) servings.

PER SERVING: 150 calories, 4 g total fat (2.5 g saturated fat), 6.5 g protein, 23.5 g carbohydrate, 15 mg cholesterol, 235 mg sodium, 3.5 g fiber.

Shining Stars

Main dishes and feature fare.

Best Dressed
Birds

Brined Roast Turkey

Poultry is perfect for a memorable holiday meal. Pick one of our succulent preparations for turkey, capon, game hens or duck.

Recipes by Liz Clark

At the holiday season in many families, turkey might well be considered the "sacred bird"! That same onion and sage stuffing that "his" mother made had better be there. Heaven forbid experimenting with wild rice and exotic mushrooms! Here we'll not touch on these unchangeable family rituals, but instead discuss how to get the most succulent bird, no matter its other components. The secret: Brine. Yes, salt water. The most common complaint when dealing with turkey is dry breast meat. A few extra days of careful planning will overcome this age old problem once and for all.

Brined Roast Turkey

The most basic ingredients—salt and water—yield an incredibly moist, tasty turkey. You'll need a big container (an extra-deep plastic dishpan will do) and some space in the refrigerator to allow the turkey to safely brine in the salt-water solution for several hours.

¾ cup kosher (coarse) salt
1 (12- to 14-lb.) fresh turkey*
2 cups reduced-sodium
   chicken broth

1 In clean nonreactive container such as plastic dishpan, add cold water to fill pan about halfway. Add salt; stir until dissolved. Place turkey in pan; add additional cold water to cover turkey. Refrigerate 24 hours, turning turkey after 12 hours to ensure that it is evenly brined.

2 Heat oven to 450°F. Place roasting rack in large roasting pan; spray rack and pan with nonstick cooking spray. Remove turkey from brine; pat dry with paper towels. If stuffing turkey, place stuffing in cavity. Tie legs together with kitchen twine; tie another piece of twine around midsection of turkey, firmly securing wings to sides. Place turkey on rack in pan, breast-side down.

3 Bake at 450°F for 30 minutes. Remove pan from oven. With oven mitts on, very carefully turn turkey breast-side up. Add chicken broth to pan. Return to oven; bake an additional 30 minutes.

4 Reduce oven temperature to 375°F. Bake 45 to 60 minutes or until

Roast Duck with Sweet Potatoes and Apples

internal temperature reaches 180°F. Baste turkey with pan drippings about every 15 minutes. Cover loosely with foil; let stand 30 minutes before carving.

TIP *A thawed frozen turkey will work as well, but avoid birds that are labeled "self basting."

10 servings.

PER SERVING: 320 calories, 16.5 g total fat (4.5 g saturated fat), 39.5 g protein, 0 g carbohydrate, 120 mg cholesterol, 830 mg sodium, 0 g fiber.

Roast Duck with Sweet Potatoes and Apples

Duck fat, a wonderfully flavorful cooking medium, is the key to the melt-in-your-mouth taste of the fruit and vegetables that accompany this moist, succulent bird. The duck cooks alone during the first half of roasting. The potatoes and apples are then added to the pan with a few table-spoons of the rendered fat, and the bird finishes roasting on top of them. This allows the duck drippings to richly flavor the fruit and vegetables.

- 4 teaspoons olive oil
- 1 (5-lb.) duck
- 1 teaspoon sea salt
- ½ teaspoon freshly ground pepper
- 4 medium sweet potatoes, peeled, cut into thin wedges*
- 4 medium Rome or Gala apples, unpeeled, cut into 8 wedges

1 Heat oven to 425°F. Place roasting rack in large roasting pan.

2 Heat oil in large skillet over medium-high heat until hot. Add duck; brown on all sides. Remove duck from skillet and place breast-side up on rack in pan. Sprinkle outside of duck with ½ teaspoon of the salt and ¼ teaspoon of the pepper. Pour about 1 inch boiling water into pan.

3 Cover and bake 30 minutes. Remove from oven. Place duck in shallow pan. Remove rack from roasting pan; pour pan drippings into heatproof bowl.

4 Place sweet potatoes and apples in same roasting pan. Sprinkle with remaining ½ teaspoon salt and ¼ teaspoon pepper. Spoon 4 tablespoons of the duck fat, which will rise to the surface of the pan drippings, over potatoes and apples. Place duck on top of potatoes and apples.

5 Cover and return to oven; bake 10 minutes. Uncover; bake an additional 25 minutes or until internal thigh temperature reaches 165°F and potatoes and apples are tender.

TIP *Look for the deep orange-colored sweet potatoes, often labeled as yams.

4 servings.

PER SERVING: 885 calories, 59.5 g total fat (19 g saturated fat), 38.5 g protein, 49 g carbohydrate, 160 mg cholesterol, 705 mg sodium, 7 g fiber.

Moister, Juicier Turkey

If you follow the standard package instructions for roasting turkey, you're likely to end up with a turkey that's bland and dry. Two techniques—soaking the turkey in salt water and cooking the turkey breast-side down for part of the roasting time—result in moister, juicier meat.

Brining Soaking the bird in salt water takes a little time and some advance planning, but it's a simple step well worth the effort. During the brining process, the turkey absorbs the salt water, resulting in a wonderfully seasoned bird from the skin right down to the bone.

Of the many styles of turkeys available during the holiday season, two are not suitable for brining. Kosher turkeys, which are coated in salt for a period of time at the processing plant, and self-basting turkeys, which have been injected with broth, fat and other seasonings, do not need to be seasoned additionally with salt. Although fresh turkeys—those that have not been deep-frozen—are preferable to frozen ones, brining greatly improves the texture and flavor of a frozen turkey.

To thaw a 12- to 14-pound frozen turkey, place it in the refrigerator 2 to 3 days before brining. If it has not completely thawed, don't worry, as it will continue to thaw in the brining solution.

Roasting If a turkey is roasted breast-side up the entire time, the breast meat cooks faster than the legs and thighs. To compound the problem, the breast meat is done at a lower internal temperature than the legs and thighs. Roasting the turkey breast-side down protects it, reducing the temperature gap between the legs and breast.

While large turkeys (those more than 15 pounds) roast more evenly

Select a container deep enough to submerge the turkey for brining.

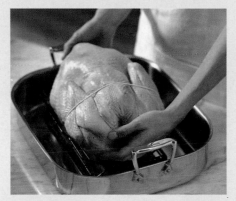
Roast the turkey breast-side down for the first 30 minutes.

After 30 minutes, carefully turn the turkey so the breast side is up.

at a lower oven temperature, small turkeys (in the 12- to 14-pound range as the one suggested here) thrive in a hot oven.

Although it is not necessary to pull out the trussing needle and perform major surgery, it is important at least to tie the turkey's legs together and secure the wings to ensure a shapely, smart-looking bird.

Crisp and Moist Duck

Duck presents a peculiar dilemma when roasting. It contains a great deal of fat just under the skin that can make the bird extremely greasy if not properly rendered. At the same time, the meat can become dry and tough once the fat is drained off. Some form of steaming or enclosed cooking, as demonstrated in the recipe for Roast Duck with Sweet Potatoes and Apples, solves the problem by surrounding the bird in a moist environment as the fat is rendered.

Before cooking the duck, remove the loose fat and trim away the excess skin with a set of good-quality poultry shears. Then, after browning the duck, place it on a rack in a roaster, adding a little boiling water to the pan to create a moist environment. Bake it, covered, to render the fat. Halfway through cooking, remove the duck from the oven to drain off the fat. Continue baking it, uncovered, to crisp the skin.

Duck also can be roasted uncovered. If you use this method, you'll need to prick the skin first to allow the fat to drain off during cooking. (Be careful, though. If the flesh is pierced in the process, the flowing meat juices from the pricked meat can cause unsightly staining on the skin.) Check the duck as it cooks and remove the accumulating fat periodically. If you don't, the duck will sizzle away in a bath of fat, which can cause it to smoke.

Many cooks prize duck fat for cooking, so you may want to save the rendered fat. Use it to cook potatoes, brown vegetables or flavor soups.

Pan-Roasted Game Hens with a Stuffing of Provençale Greens

Pan-Roasted Game Hens with a Stuffing of Provençale Greens

Cornish game hens are filled with an incredible sweet-savory stuffing that's based on a classic French Swiss chard pie (spinach stands in for the Swiss chard). It's a wonderful way to keep the little hens, which have a tendency to dry out, extremely moist, and it allows for a festive presentation.

STUFFING
- ½ cup raisins
- ¼ cup boiling water
- 1 lb. baby spinach leaves
- 2 Golden Delicious apples, unpeeled, finely chopped
- ½ cup (2 oz.) freshly grated Parmesan cheese
- ⅓ cup pine nuts, toasted
- ¼ cup sugar
- 2 teaspoons grated orange peel
- ¼ teaspoon freshly grated nutmeg
- ¼ teaspoon freshly ground pepper
- 1 egg, beaten

GAME HENS
- 6 (24-oz.) Cornish game hens
- 1 teaspoon sea salt
- ¼ teaspoon freshly ground pepper
- 2 tablespoons olive oil
- 2 cups reduced-sodium chicken broth

1 In small bowl, combine raisins and boiling water; let stand 10 minutes or until raisins are soft. Drain; set aside.

2 Meanwhile, blanch spinach by cooking in boiling, salted water 30 to 60 seconds or until wilted. Drain. Cool and squeeze to remove excess moisture; coarsely chop.

3 In large bowl, combine spinach, raisins and all remaining stuffing ingredients; mix well.

4 Sprinkle cavity and outside of game hens with salt and ¼ teaspoon pepper. Stuff each hen with ⅙ of spinach mixture. Tie legs of each hen together with kitchen twine; tie another piece of twine around midsection of each hen, firmly securing wings to sides of hen.

5 Heat large skillet over medium-high heat until hot. Add oil; heat until hot. Brown game hens in batches 5 to 10 minutes or until browned on all sides. Place hens in single layer, breast-side up, in large roasting pan or Dutch oven.

6 Place skillet over medium-high heat. Add chicken broth; bring to a boil, scraping up any browned bits from bottom of pan. Pour broth over hens.

7 Place roasting pan with hens over medium-high heat; cover. Bring broth to a boil; reduce heat to medium-low or low to maintain a gentle simmer. Cook 1¼ to 1½ hours or until internal temperature reaches 180°F. Remove twine before serving. Strain pan juices; skim off fat. Serve with pan juices.

6 servings.

PER SERVING: 855 calories, 55 g total fat (15 g saturated fat), 61 g protein, 30 g carbohydrate, 345 mg cholesterol, 820 mg sodium, 4 g fiber.

Roast Capon with Chestnut-Polenta Croutons

The capon is an ideal choice for the holiday dinner that demands something more festive than a chicken but not as large as a turkey. This fat male bird makes an elegant showing on a platter. The fresh sage is very Italian, and the chestnuts added to the polenta are reminiscent of the Piedmont and Lombardy regions of Italy.

CAPON
- 1 (8-lb.) capon
- 15 fresh sage leaves
- 1 teaspoon sea salt
- ¼ teaspoon freshly ground pepper
- 2 small carrots, cut into ½-inch slices
- 2 ribs celery, leaves included, cut into 3-inch pieces
- 1 medium onion, cut into 8 pieces

CROUTONS
- 5 cups reduced-sodium chicken broth
- ¼ cup butter

Serving Cornish Game Hens

Cornish game hens are perfect for holiday entertaining. They cook relatively quickly, they're festive, and because they're often served whole, carving is left to the diner, not the cook.

Because they're so small, however, these birds often overcook before they've had a chance to brown. To solve this problem, our Pan-Roasted Game Hens (opposite page) are browned stovetop, then covered and roasted stovetop as well.

If you plan to serve one hen per person, try to find the smallest ones possible, preferably 1½ pounds or less. If the only available hens are much over the 1½ pound size, you may want to consider serving one hen for every two guests. Cornish hens are relatively easy to split before serving. Using a pair of heavy-duty poultry shears, cut along the breast bone. Once the birds are halved along the breast, the final cut along the backbone is simple.

Poussins, or baby chickens, are usually smaller (if more expensive) options to Cornish game hens. They are often available in supermarkets, and certainly by mail, around the holidays. Though similar in flavor, poussins are baby chickens, while Cornish game hens are dwarfed birds—a cross of Plymouth Rock and Cornish hens.

As with turkey and other poultry, it is not necessary to elaborately truss these little birds. Simply tie their legs together and secure their wings for a shapely, attractive presentation.

Roast Capon with
Chestnut-Polenta Croutons

1½ cups cornmeal
2 cups canned chestnuts, drained, coarsely chopped
1 cup (4 oz.) freshly grated Parmesan cheese
¼ cup chopped fresh sage

1 Heat oven to 450°F. Place roasting rack in large roasting pan; spray rack and pan with nonstick cooking spray. With your fingers, gently loosen skin from breast of capon, beginning at neck cavity and working toward the thigh, being very careful not to break through skin. Place 12 of the sage leaves under skin of bird.

2 Sprinkle salt and pepper in cavity and on outside of bird. Place remaining 3 sage leaves, carrots, celery and onion in cavity. Tie legs together with kitchen twine; tie another piece of twine around midsection of bird, firmly securing wings to sides of bird. Skewer neck skin to back of bird with wooden skewer. Place bird, breast-side down, on rack in roasting pan.

3 Bake at 450°F for 30 minutes. Remove pan from oven. Grasping bird with oven mitts, turn bird breast-side up. Reduce oven temperature to 375°F. Bake an additional 40 to 50 minutes or until internal temperature reaches 170°F to 175°F.

4 Meanwhile, spray 15x10x1-inch pan and baking sheet with nonstick cooking spray.

5 In large saucepan, bring chicken broth and butter to a boil over medium heat. Whisking constantly, slowly pour cornmeal into broth. Continue cooking 10 minutes. Stir in chestnuts, cheese and sage. Pour polenta into pan; smooth with spatula. Refrigerate 35 to 40 minutes or until firm enough to cut. Cut polenta into 12 squares; cut each diagonally to form 24 triangles. Place triangles on baking sheet. (Polenta can be made up to 1 day ahead. Cover and refrigerate.)

6 Remove capon from oven; place on serving platter. Cover loosely with foil; let stand 20 to 30 minutes before carving. Meanwhile, heat broiler. Broil polenta 4 to 6 inches from heat 2 to 4 minutes or until golden brown, turning once, watching carefully to avoid burning. Arrange chestnut-polenta croutons around capon. Garnish with sprigs of fresh sage.

8 servings.

PER SERVING: 725 calories, 35 g total fat (13.5 g saturated fat), 66 g protein, 33 g carbohydrate, 195 mg cholesterol, 1060 mg sodium, 4 g fiber.

Just-Right Capon

For holiday dinners where a 4-pound chicken is too small and a 14-pound turkey is too large, an 8-pound capon may, in fact, be the perfect size.

A capon is simply a castrated male chicken. His loss translates into weight gains upwards of 10 pounds before slaughter. The last week or so before processing, a capon is fed milk and bread, resulting in meat that is extraordinarily white in color and sweet in taste.

The turkey and capon have much in common. Like the turkey, a capon can be brined, and its breast meat is particularly juicy when roasted breast-side down for part of the cooking time. And, tying its legs together and securing its wings guarantees a more festive-looking bird.

A capon roasting breast-side down on a wire rack can be precarious. A V-rack, however, safely and effectively holds the capon (as well as all other birds that are started breast side down) in place. To easily rotate a capon, use a wad of paper toweling in each hand or oven mitts (if you don't mind getting them dirty).

Serves
Two

Personal Meat Loaves

Small is beautiful (and delicious) in these pared-down entrees.

Text and Recipes by Melanie Barnard

For 25 years, I cooked for a crowd. Three strapping sons and their hungry friends made a revolving door of my refrigerator. Those were the days when grocery shopping was, by necessity, a major daily event, and quantity was the overriding factor in my cooking. Recipes were routinely doubled to ensure everyone had enough to eat.

Now that the kids are gone, I'm usually trying to reduce a recipe. Unfortunately, it's often harder to cut a recipe in half than it is to double it. These recipes are the perfect solution: They serve just two. You can make just what you can eat and won't be burdened with unwanted leftovers. And if the kids come home for dinner, the recipes can easily be doubled.

Personal Meat Loaves

The real advantage in having your own "personal" meat loaf is not having to share the coveted, crusty end pieces with anyone! Serve with mashed or baked potatoes and steamed green beans, or pick up on the loaves' Southwestern flavor by stirring green onions, corn and sour cream into the potatoes and sprinkling the beans with finely diced pimiento or roasted red bell pepper. Most supermarkets carry a meat loaf mix of lean ground beef, pork and veal. You can substitute ground turkey with good results too.

 1 tablespoon olive oil
 ½ cup chopped onion
 1 tablespoon chili powder
 ½ teaspoon ground cumin
 10 oz. lean ground meat loaf
     mix (equal parts ground
     beef, pork and veal)
 ¼ cup unseasoned dry bread
     crumbs
 ¼ cup chopped fresh cilantro
 ½ teaspoon salt
 ¼ teaspoon freshly ground pepper
 1 egg
 2 tablespoons hickory-smoked
     barbecue sauce

1 Heat oven to 350°F. Heat oil in small skillet over medium heat until hot. Add onion; cook 5 minutes or until softened, stirring frequently. Add chili powder and cumin; cook 1 minute. Remove from heat; cool 5 minutes.

2 In medium bowl, combine ground meat, bread crumbs, cilantro, salt, pepper, egg and cooked onion mixture. With hands, mix gently but thoroughly.

Shrimp and Fennel over Linguine

3 Divide mixture in half. Shape each half into free-form loaf about 4 inches long. Place in shallow glass baking dish or pie plate. Spread tops with barbecue sauce. (Recipe can be prepared up to 4 hours ahead. Cover and refrigerate. An additional 5 to 10 minutes baking time may be needed if meat loaf mixture has been refrigerated.)

4 Bake 35 to 45 minutes or until no longer pink in center.

2 servings.

PER SERVING: 440 calories, 26.5 g total fat (8 g saturated fat), 31.5 g protein, 18 g carbohydrate, 195 mg cholesterol, 965 mg sodium, 3 g fiber.

Shrimp and Fennel over Linguine

Scallops also pair well with fennel and can replace shrimp in this dish, as could calamari or even lobster meat if you have a cause for celebration. Shellfish cook very quickly, so whatever option you use, add it at the very end. Complete this simple supper with an arugula salad tossed with a creamy Gorgonzola dressing, and serve a basket of crusty Italian bread.

1   tablespoon olive oil
1   cup thinly sliced fennel
      bulb, fronds removed
1   cup coarsely chopped onion
3   large garlic cloves, minced
¼   teaspoon salt
¼   to ½ teaspoon crushed
      red pepper
1   (14½-oz.) can Italian-style
      diced tomatoes, undrained
⅓   to ½ cup white wine
      or bottled clam juice
½   lb. shelled, deveined
      uncooked medium shrimp
¼   cup chopped fresh basil
¼   cup chopped fresh Italian parsley
4½ oz. fresh linguine
      (from 9-oz. pkg.)*

1 Heat oil in large skillet over medium heat until hot. Add fennel and onion; cook 5 to 6 minutes or until softened, stirring frequently.

2 Stir in garlic, salt and crushed red pepper. Cook 1 minute. Add tomatoes and ⅓ cup wine. Simmer, uncovered, 5 minutes or until slightly thickened. If mixture seems too thick, add remaining wine. Gently stir in shrimp, basil and parsley. Cook 3 minutes or until shrimp turn pink.

3 Meanwhile, cook linguine according to package directions; drain well. Toss linguine with hot shrimp mixture.

TIP *Freeze remaining linguine for a later use.

2 servings.

PER SERVING: 520 calories, 9.5 g total fat (1.5 g saturated fat), 30 g protein, 78.5 g carbohydrate, 160 mg cholesterol, 1350 mg sodium, 7 g fiber.

Mixed Mushroom and Tarragon Risotto

Use whatever fresh mushroom combination looks good at your market. Dried mushrooms also can be used. Reconstitute them by covering them with boiling water and then letting them stand until plumped and tender, which usually takes about 20 minutes. Don't discard any remaining liquid, but instead strain it through a fine strainer or cheesecloth to remove any mushroom impurities; then add the liquid to the simmering broth mixture. Risotto is a one-dish meal, needing only a mixed green salad with a tart red wine vinaigrette to round it out.

3   cups reduced-sodium
      vegetable or chicken broth
1   cup white wine or 1 cup
      additional vegetable broth
2   tablespoons butter
2   cups (about 8 oz.) sliced
      mixed mushrooms, such as
      shiitake, portobello and button
1   cup thinly sliced leeks (white
      and pale green parts only)
1   cup Arborio rice
¼   teaspoon freshly ground pepper
1   tablespoon chopped fresh
      tarragon
¼   cup (1 oz.) freshly grated
      Parmesan cheese

1 In medium saucepan, bring broth and wine to a simmer.

2 Meanwhile, melt 1 tablespoon of the butter in heavy large saucepan over medium heat. Add mushrooms; cook 3 to 5 minutes or until softened, stirring frequently. Remove mushrooms from saucepan with slotted spoon; set aside.

3 Add remaining 1 tablespoon butter and leeks to saucepan; cook until softened, stirring frequently. Add rice and pepper; cook about 1 minute, stirring, until rice is coated. Add all but ½ cup of the simmering broth mixture. Reduce heat to medium-low; cook 18 to 20 minutes or until rice has absorbed most of the liquid and is tender, stirring frequently.

4 Stir in tarragon and mushrooms. Cook 2 minutes, stirring constantly. Add cheese; stir to blend. If necessary, add remaining broth for a creamy consistency.

2 servings.

PER SERVING: 575 calories, 16.5 g total fat (10 g saturated fat), 15 g protein, 88 g carbohydrate, 40 mg cholesterol, 710 mg sodium, 3.5 g fiber.

Curried Lamb Chops with Mint Pesto Raita

Commercial curry powder loses its flavor quickly. If the jar on your shelf is more than six months old, invest in a new one. Serve these chops with boiled small red or Yukon gold potatoes and broiled tomato slices.

RAITA
1   cup lightly packed fresh
      mint leaves
2   large garlic cloves
3   tablespoons pine nuts
1   tablespoon fresh lemon juice
¼   teaspoon salt
¼   teaspoon freshly ground pepper
3   tablespoons olive oil
¼   cup low-fat plain yogurt

Peppered Pork with Mustard Fruit Compote

LAMB CHOPS

6 rib or loin lamb chops
(about 2½ oz. each)
2 teaspoons curry powder
¼ teaspoon salt
¼ teaspoon freshly ground pepper

1 Place mint leaves in food processor. With machine running, add garlic cloves; process until finely chopped. Add pine nuts; process until finely chopped. Add lemon juice, ¼ teaspoon salt and ¼ teaspoon pepper; process 30 seconds or until blended. (Mixture should still have some texture.) With machine running, slowly add oil. Add yogurt; pulse just to combine. (Raita can be made up to 1 day ahead. Cover and refrigerate. Bring to room temperature before serving.)

2 Heat broiler. Sprinkle both sides of lamb chops with curry powder, ¼ teaspoon salt and ¼ teaspoon pepper; place in small broiler pan or shallow pan. Broil 4 to 5 inches from heat 6 to 8 minutes for medium-rare to medium, turning once.

3 Arrange 3 chops on each plate. Spoon raita over chops.

2 servings.

PER SERVING: 450 calories, 37.5 g total fat (7.5 g saturated fat), 23 g protein, 8 g carbohydrate, 65 mg cholesterol, 675 mg sodium, 2.5 g fiber.

Peppered Pork with Mustard Fruit Compote

Pork and fruit are naturally complementary. As with all savory fruit dishes, it's important to temper sweetness—the black pepper coating and mustard seasoning do the trick nicely. The tenderloin is indeed the most tender and delicate cut of pork, but it also can dry out quickly if overcooked, so watch it carefully. The pork is wonderful served with sautéed broccoli rabe and noodles tossed with butter and poppy seeds.

PORK

1 (8- to 12-oz.) pork tenderloin
1 tablespoon olive oil
2 teaspoons coarsely ground pepper
¼ teaspoon salt

COMPOTE

¾ cup (6 oz.) quartered mixed pitted prunes and dried apricots
⅔ cup apple juice
4½ teaspoons fresh lemon juice
1 tablespoon Dijon mustard
3 tablespoons thinly sliced green onions

1 Heat oven to 425°F. Brush entire surface of pork with oil. Sprinkle with pepper and salt, pressing pepper into pork. Place in ungreased small shallow pan.

2 Bake 15 to 20 minutes or until internal temperature reaches 150°F. Loosely cover; let stand 10 minutes before serving.

3 Meanwhile, in medium saucepan, stir together fruit, apple juice, lemon juice and mustard. Simmer over medium heat 10 to 15 minutes or until fruit is soft and juices are glossy and thickened, stirring frequently. (Compote can be made up to 1 day ahead. Cool, cover and refrigerate. Heat before serving, adding about 2 tablespoons additional apple juice to thin compote, if necessary.) Stir in 2 tablespoons of the green onions.

4 Slice pork diagonally into ½-inch slices; place on serving platter. Sprinkle with remaining green onions. Serve pork with compote.

2 servings.

PER SERVING: 385 calories, 11.5 g total fat (2.5 g saturated fat), 26.5 g protein, 47 g carbohydrate, 65 mg cholesterol, 445 mg sodium, 5.5 g fiber.

(Clockwise from top left) Yemenite Chile Sauce,
Mesquite-Grilled Tomato Salsa with Chiles de Arbo,
Afghani Coriander-Walnut Chutney

Revved-up sauces get their heat from an international cast of chiles.

Text and Recipes by Steven Raichlen

When it's hot, it's hot. I'm talking about a quartet of fiendishly fiery sauces that is guaranteed to set your next barbecue on fire. The incendiary agents in these sauces are chiles. But there's more to these edible flamethrowers than heat. Even the world's hottest chile, the Caribbean Scotch bonnet, has a delicate floral apricot flavor behind its ferocious bite. Mexico's chile de árbol boasts a subtle smoky taste that goes great with grilled steaks.

These four sauces come from all over the world of barbecue: the smoky Mango-Scotch Bonnet Barbecue Sauce is inspired by the Caribbean; the tongue-torturing Mesquite-Grilled Tomato Salsa with Chiles de Arbol comes from Mexico; the cumin-scented Yemenite Chile Sauce hails from Israel; and the pungent Afghani Coriander-Walnut Chutney has its roots in Afghanistan. All of them are great with grilled seafood, poultry and meats. In addition, you can use three of the sauces for basting as well as for serving.

So break out the beer (or Pepto-Bismol) and let the fireworks begin!

Yemenite Chile Sauce

This is Israel's national barbecue sauce—a diabolical blend of chiles, garlic and cumin with just enough tomato and olive oil to keep you from setting your tongue on fire. Serve this sauce with grilled fish, or beef or lamb shish kabobs, and have plenty of drinks on hand to extinguish the fire.

    2   tomatoes, peeled, seeded
    5   garlic cloves, coarsely chopped
    4 to 6 jalapeño chiles,
          seeded, coarsely chopped*
    ¼   cup chopped fresh cilantro
    1   teaspoon salt
    1   teaspoon ground cumin
    ½   teaspoon freshly ground pepper
    ⅓   cup extra-virgin olive oil
    3   tablespoons fresh lemon juice

Combine all ingredients in blender or food processor; blend to form smooth sauce.

TIP *For hotter sauce, do not remove seeds.

2 cups.

PER 2 TABLESPOONS: 45 calories, 4.5 g total fat (.5 g saturated fat), .5 g protein, 1.5 g carbohydrate, 0 mg cholesterol, 150 mg sodium, .5 g fiber.

Mesquite-Grilled Tomato Salsa with Chiles de Arbol

This fiery salsa does double duty in northern Mexico—first as a dip for chips, then as a smoke-scented accompaniment to grilled steaks. Its distinctive smoke flavor comes from grilling the main ingredients over mesquite. The fire power comes from the long, slender chiles de árbol, available dried at Mexican markets and many gourmet shops. Use two for mild heat, six if you have a stomach of steel. You could also make the salsa with chipotle chiles (smoked jalapeño chiles), which add a smoke flavor all their own. Serve the salsa over beef or tuna steaks.

2 cups mesquite wood chips
2 to 6 chiles de árbol or 1 to
    3 chipotle chiles*
2 large tomatoes
1 small onion, halved
2 garlic cloves, chopped
3 tablespoons coarsely
    chopped fresh cilantro
2 tablespoons fresh lime juice
½ teaspoon salt
¼ teaspoon freshly ground pepper

1 Soak wood chips 1 hour in cold water to cover; drain. Place chiles in small bowl of warm water; let stand 20 to 30 minutes or until pliable. Drain; remove and discard seeds. (For spicier salsa, do not remove seeds.)

2 Meanwhile, heat grill. If using charcoal grill, place wood chips on coals. If using gas grill, place wood chips in smoker box following manufacturer's instructions. Or wrap chips in foil; make holes in package with pencil. Place package over one of burners under grate.

3 When thick cloud of smoke forms, place tomatoes and onion on grill. Cook 6 to 8 minutes or until skins are charred and blistered on all sides; cool.

4 Place chiles, tomatoes, onion, garlic and cilantro in food processor or blender; puree to form coarse paste. Stir in lime juice, salt and pepper.

TIP *Chile de árbol is a long, smooth, thin dried chile with a bright-red color. Chipotle chiles are brown, dried, smoked jalapeño chiles with wrinkled skin.

2 cups.

PER ¼ CUP: 15 calories, 0 g total fat (0 g saturated fat), .5 g protein, 3.5 g carbohydrate, 0 mg cholesterol, 155 mg sodium, 1 g fiber.

Afghani Coriander-Walnut Chutney

Order kabobs in Afghanistan, Pakistan or northern India, and you'll be served some version of this soulful chutney. Chiles give it heat. Fresh cilantro makes it aromatic. Ground walnuts give it a richness that will have you rushing back for seconds. Try it with grilled chicken, lamb or seafood, or even as a dip.

1 cup chopped fresh cilantro
½ cup chopped walnuts
4 garlic cloves, coarsely chopped
1 to 3 jalapeño chiles,
    seeded, coarsely chopped*
¼ cup coarsely chopped onion
2 tablespoons fresh lemon juice
2 tablespoons red wine vinegar
2 tablespoons olive oil
1 teaspoon salt
½ teaspoon ground cumin
½ teaspoon freshly ground pepper
¼ teaspoon sugar
4 to 5 tablespoons cold water

Combine all ingredients in blender; blend, scraping down sides of blender a few times and adding additional 1 tablespoon water, as needed, to form a pourable sauce.

TIP *For hotter chutney, do not remove seeds.

1 cup.

PER 2 TABLESPOONS: 85 calories, 8 g total fat (1 g saturated fat), 1.5 g protein, 3.5 g carbohydrate, 0 mg cholesterol, 300 mg sodium, 1 g fiber.

Mango-Scotch Bonnet Barbecue Sauce

Mark Militello, chef-owner of Mark's South Beach on Miami Beach and Mark's Las Olas in Fort Lauderdale, created this fiery, smoky sauce after a sojourn in the French West Indies. It's everything a barbecue sauce should be—sweet, tart, fruity, fiery and smoky. It's made with Scotch bonnets, the chile of choice in the West Indies and the hottest chile around. Scotch bonnets are similar in appearance to habaneros, which can be substituted.

2 cups oak or hickory wood chips
2 tomatoes
1 green bell pepper
1 red bell pepper
1 small onion, halved
1 large mango, peeled, seeded,
    diced (about 2 cups)
1 to 3 Scotch bonnet or
    habanero chiles, halved
3 large garlic cloves, minced
½ cup packed brown sugar
1 teaspoon ground cumin
1 teaspoon dried thyme
½ teaspoon cinnamon
½ teaspoon freshly ground pepper
¼ teaspoon salt
½ cup water
⅓ cup cider vinegar
2 tablespoons Dijon mustard
2 tablespoons molasses
2 tablespoons fresh lime juice

1 Soak wood chips 1 hour in water to cover; drain. Meanwhile, heat grill. If using charcoal grill, place wood chips on coals. If using gas grill, place chips in smoker box following manufacturer's instructions. Or wrap chips in foil; make holes in package with pencil. Place package over one of burners under grate.

2 When thick cloud of smoke forms, place tomatoes, green bell pepper, red bell pepper and onion on grill. Cook 6 to 8 minutes or until skins are charred and blistered on all sides. Place vegetables on cutting board; cool.

3 Scrape off charred skin and remove seeds and core from bell peppers. Finely chop vegetables.

4 Place in large saucepan. Add all remaining ingredients; partially cover. Bring to a boil over medium heat; reduce heat to low. Gently simmer, uncovered, 20 minutes, stirring occasionally and adding additional water as needed to keep ingredients moist. Cool slightly.

5 Blend sauce in blender in batches until smooth. Press through sieve or strainer into medium bowl.

3 cups.

PER ¼ CUP: 80 calories, .5 g total fat (0 g saturated fat), 1 g protein, 20 g carbohydrate, 0 mg cholesterol, 120 mg sodium, .5 g fiber.

Chiles for Hot Sauces

chile de árbol

chipotle

habanero

jalapeño

serrano

thai

Chiles, the fiery members of the pepper family, give a cutting edge to barbecue sauces and marinades. Here's a scorecard to help you know the players. If you can't find the chiles locally, two good sources are Melissa's (www.melissas.com or 800-588-0151) or Frieda's (www.friedas.com or 800-241-1771).

One note of caution: Wear rubber gloves when handling chiles because the oil can linger on your skin even after washing. The hottest parts of chiles are the seeds and veins. Cut chiles in half, and scrape out the seeds and veins with a paring knife or grapefruit spoon. Leave in the seeds and veins only if you want the added heat.

Cayenne A small (2 inches long), fiery, red chile native to the Gulf of Mexico and now widely grown throughout Africa, India and Asia. Cayenne is very hot, but its flavor is fairly one-dimensional. It's most often used in powdered form.

Chile de árbol A long (3 to 4 inches), slender, red chile from Mexico. It's dried and moderately fiery; it's used in the charred tomato salsas that accompany grilled beef in northern Mexico.

Chipotle These smoked jalapeño chiles are from Mexico. They're available dried or canned. The canned are packed in a flavorful vinegar sauce called adobo.

Habanero This is Mexico's version of the Scotch bonnet chile. It is smooth, acorn-shaped, and red, green or yellow in color. It takes its name from the Spanish word for Havana.

Jalapeño This bullet-shaped green or red pepper with gentle heat and grassy flavor is widely available.

Scotch bonnet It's shaped like a Chinese lantern and 50 times hotter than a jalapeño, but behind the heat, there's a smoky, fruity flavor that may remind you of apricots. It's sold at West Indian markets, specialty produce stores and some supermarkets. You can substitute habaneros if you can't find Scotch bonnets.

Serrano This is a thin, tapered, bright-green chile that's smaller and slightly hotter than a jalapeño. The two can be used interchangeably.

Thai Two peppers are sold under the name Thai chile. The prik kee noo is a tiny, ridged, mercilessly hot version whose name in Thai means "mouse dropping." The prik kee far is a slender, horn-shaped, green chile that is very hot but milder than the prik kee noo. Look for Thai chiles at Asian and Indian markets, or substitute milder serrano or jalapeño chiles.

Fire and
Pork

All-American BBQ Pork Sandwich

Pork tenderloin's naturally tender nature makes it a great choice for the grill.

Text and Recipes by Melanie Barnard

You might not think it to look at it, but pork tenderloin is packed with power—grill power, that is. This cut of meat, shaped like a log, is naturally lean, tender and moist, so it can stand up to the grill's high heat.

Pork tenderloin cooks fast, so it's perfect for quick weeknight meals. Yet its flavor and versatility make it an ideal entree for weekend entertaining. Season it with marinades or rubs. Cook it whole, butterflied, rolled or skewered. Its mild yet distinctive taste and buttery texture partners well with various seasonings and accompaniments, as well as the flavors that come from the fire.

For fast-cooking, rich-tasting entrees, reach for pork tenderloin—and light the coals.

All-American BBQ Pork Sandwiches

Sweet, spicy and vinegary, this hearty sandwich features the best of American barbecue flavor in a fraction of the time. That's because it uses quick-cooking pork tenderloin. Serve it in the Carolina style—on buns with creamy coleslaw on the side or spooned onto the sandwich. For even more authentic flavor, toss hickory chips on the fire.

PORK
1 (about 1-lb.) pork tenderloin
1 sweet onion, sliced (½ inch)
1 tablespoon vegetable oil
2 teaspoons celery seeds
2 teaspoons packed brown sugar
4 teaspoons paprika
½ teaspoon salt
¼ teaspoon freshly ground pepper
¼ cup water
1 tablespoon cider vinegar
¼ teaspoon hot pepper sauce

SAUCE
½ cup hickory smoke-flavored barbecue sauce
1 tablespoon cider vinegar
1 tablespoon bourbon, if desired
¼ to ½ teaspoon hot pepper sauce

BUNS
4 sandwich buns, split

1 Heat grill. Brush pork tenderloin and onion slices with oil. In small bowl, stir together celery seeds, brown sugar, paprika, salt and pepper. Press mixture onto pork tenderloin and both sides of onion slices.

Pork Tenderloin Saté

1 (about 1-lb.) pork
    tenderloin, cut into
    1½-inch cubes
    (about 12 pieces)
2 tablespoons sesame seeds
1 tablespoon dark sesame oil
8 cups mixed salad greens
    or baby spinach leaves
¼ cup chopped peanuts
¼ cup thinly sliced green onions

1 In resealable plastic bag, mix together ¼ cup of the vinegar, soy sauce, peanut butter, molasses, ginger and garlic until smooth. Reserve 6 tablespoons in small bowl for dressing. Add pork to remaining marinade; stir to coat all sides. Seal bag; refrigerate at least 15 minutes or up to 1 hour.

2 Heat grill. Thread pork onto 4 (8- to 10-inch) metal skewers. Sprinkle with sesame seeds.

3 When ready to grill, oil grill rack. Place pork on gas grill over medium heat or on charcoal grill 4 to 6 inches from medium coals. Cook 8 to 10 minutes or until slightly pink in center, turning occasionally.

4 Meanwhile, whisk reserved marinade with remaining 1 tablespoon vinegar and sesame oil.

5 In large bowl, toss salad greens with enough dressing to coat greens. Divide among 4 plates. Arrange skewered pork on salads. Sprinkle with peanuts and green onions. Drizzle with remaining dressing.

4 servings.

PER SERVING: 305 calories, 17 g total fat (3.5 g saturated fat), 27 g protein, 13 g carbohydrate, 55 mg cholesterol, 610 mg sodium, 4 g fiber.

2 In small bowl, combine water, 1 tablespoon vinegar and ¼ teaspoon hot pepper sauce.

3 When ready to grill, oil grill rack. Place pork on gas grill over medium heat or on charcoal grill 4 to 6 inches from medium coals. Cook 15 to 20 minutes or until internal temperature reaches 145°F, turning and brushing occasionally with vinegar mixture.

4 Meanwhile, place onion slices on grill; cook 8 to 10 minutes or until softened and charred at edges, turning occasionally.

5 Place pork and onions on cutting board. Loosely cover with foil; let stand 10 minutes.

6 Meanwhile, in small saucepan, stir together all sauce ingredients. Cook over medium to medium-low heat 5 minutes, stirring occasionally. (Sauce can be made up to 2 days ahead. Cover and refrigerate. Reheat before use.)

7 To serve, thinly slice pork and separate onion into rings; place in medi- um bowl. Add sauce; toss to coat. Spoon pork and onion into buns.

4 sandwiches.

PER SANDWICH: 330 calories, 10 g total fat (2.5 g saturated fat), 24.5 g protein, 33 g carbohydrate, 55 mg cholesterol, 835 mg sodium, 3 g fiber.

Pork Tenderloin Saté

Inspired by classic Indonesian saté, this salad makes a lovely, light summertime main course. The vinaigrette is simply an enhancement of the flavoring sauce for the pork. If you use bamboo skewers, be sure to soak them in cold water for at least 20 minutes first.

¼ cup plus 1 tablespoon rice
    wine vinegar
3 tablespoons soy sauce
3 tablespoons creamy peanut butter
2 tablespoons molasses
1 tablespoon finely chopped
    fresh ginger
2 garlic cloves, finely chopped

Tandoor-Style Pork Tenderloin

Yogurt flavors the pork, but it also acts as a protective coating, keeping it moist and juicy during grilling. The yogurt is seasoned with garam masala, a mix of spices commonly used in Indian cooking and now available in the spice section of many supermarkets. Serve this dish with basmati rice, steamed zucchini, and Indian chutneys or raita (a seasoned yogurt dip).

2 (¾-lb.) pork tenderloins
1 cup low-fat plain yogurt
⅓ cup finely chopped onion
2 tablespoons lemon juice
5 teaspoons garam masala*
½ teaspoon salt

1 Butterfly each pork tenderloin by cutting lengthwise down center without cutting all the way through.

2 In shallow dish just large enough to hold pork or in resealable plastic bag, mix together all remaining ingredients. Add pork; turn to coat. Cover dish or seal bag; refrigerate 30 minutes or up to 2 hours, turning occasionally.

3 Heat grill. When ready to grill, remove pork from marinade; discard marinade. Oil grill rack; place pork on gas grill over medium heat or on charcoal grill 4 to 6 inches from medium coals. Cook 13 to 16 minutes or until internal temperature reaches 145°F, turning occasionally. Place pork on serving platter. Loosely cover with foil; let stand about 10 minutes. To serve, slice pork diagonally.

TIP *If garam masala is unavailable, place 2 cinnamon sticks and 1 whole nutmeg in heavy plastic bag. With meat mallet or heavy saucepan, crush cinnamon and nutmeg into coarse pieces. Place cinnamon and nutmeg pieces, 2 tablespoons cumin seeds, 1 tablespoon coriander seeds, 1 tablespoon whole cardamom, 2 teaspoons black peppercorns and 1 teaspoon whole cloves in clean, dry coffee or spice grinder; grind to a fine powder. Mixture can be stored in airtight jar 3 to 4 months.

6 servings.

PER SERVING: 160 calories, 4.5 g total fat (1.5 g saturated fat), 26 g protein, 1.5 g carbohydrate, 70 mg cholesterol, 105 mg sodium, .5 g fiber.

Curried Pork with Pineapple-Chipotle Chutney

Pork has a natural affinity for fruit, so it's paired here with a sweet, hot and delicious compote of bottled chutney, fresh pineapple and smoky chipotle chiles. Chipotle chiles, which are smoked jalapeño chiles, are canned in a spicy adobo sauce and are usually shelved in the ethnic section of large supermarkets.

PORK
2 (¾-lb.) pork tenderloins
1 cup pineapple juice
2 tablespoons curry powder
1 teaspoon salt
½ teaspoon cayenne pepper

CHUTNEY
1 cup purchased mango chutney
1 cup diced fresh pineapple
½ cup diced red bell pepper
½ cup pineapple juice
2 finely chopped chipotle chiles in adobo sauce
2 teaspoons adobo sauce

1 Butterfly each pork tenderloin by cutting lengthwise down center without cutting all the way through.

2 In shallow dish just large enough to hold pork or in resealable plastic bag, mix together 1 cup pineapple juice, curry powder, salt and pepper. Add pork; turn to coat. Cover dish or seal bag; refrigerate at least 1 hour or up to 8 hours, turning frequently.

3 Heat grill. When ready to grill, remove pork from marinade; discard marinade. Oil grill rack; place pork on gas grill over medium heat or on charcoal grill 4 to 6 inches from medium coals. Cook 13 to 16 minutes or until internal temperature reaches 145°F, turning occasionally. Place pork on serving platter. Cover with foil; let stand about 10 minutes.

4 Meanwhile, in small saucepan, stir together all chutney ingredients. Bring to a boil over medium-high heat. Reduce heat to low; simmer 10 minutes. (Chutney can be made up to 8 hours ahead. Cover and refrigerate. Reheat before use.)

5 To serve, slice pork diagonally. Serve with warm chutney.

6 servings.

PER SERVING: 245 calories, 4.5 g total fat (1.5 g saturated fat), 26 g protein, 24.5 g carbohydrate, 70 mg cholesterol, 350 mg sodium, 1.5 g fiber.

Curried Pork with Pineapple-Chipotle Chutney

How to Butterfly

Pork tenderloin can be butterflied to create a wider, thinner piece of meat. Cut this way, it cooks quicker; it's also suitable for stuffing and rolling.

To butterfly a tenderloin, make a lengthwise cut down the center of the meat, being careful not to cut all the way through. Spread open the meat like a book—or a butterfly—and flatten it slightly. (The meat also can be cut lengthwise from the side of the tenderloin, with the knife running parallel to the cutting board.)

Peppered Pork Stuffed with Orange and Tarragon

This pretty rolled tenderloin is bursting with an orange-herbal flavor. Other herbs, such as thyme or sage, can be substituted for the tarragon. If you'd like to add a bit of flavor to the fire, good choices are orange rinds or grapevine cuttings (soak the vine first for about 20 minutes).

PORK
- 2 (¾-lb.) pork tenderloins
- ¼ cup finely chopped shallots
- 3 tablespoons grated orange peel
- 3 tablespoons chopped fresh tarragon
- 2 tablespoons extra-virgin olive oil
- 4 teaspoons cracked black peppercorns
- 1 teaspoon sea or kosher (coarse) salt

SAUCE
- ½ cup orange juice
- 2 tablespoons chopped fresh tarragon
- 2 tablespoons coarse-grain Dijon mustard
- 2 tablespoons extra-virgin olive oil

1 Butterfly each pork tenderloin by cutting lengthwise down center without cutting all the way through.

2 Sprinkle cut side of each tenderloin with shallots, orange peel and 3 tablespoons tarragon. Roll each tenderloin, starting with the long edge. Tie in 3 or 4 places with kitchen twine. Brush each tenderloin with 1 tablespoon of the oil. Sprinkle with peppercorns and salt; press onto pork. Let stand 10 minutes at room temperature, or cover and refrigerate up to 1 hour.

3 Heat grill. When ready to grill, oil grill rack. Place pork on gas grill over medium heat or on charcoal grill 4 to 6 inches from medium coals. Cook 15 to 18 minutes or until

Is It Done Yet?

Pork tenderloin, like its beef counterpart, is a tender, lean and expensive cut of meat. Properly cooked, it is moist, juicy and altogether sensational. Overcooked, it is pricey shoe leather. Because grilling is an imprecise and variable cooking method, it's especially important to be able to determine when the meat is done.

If the tenderloin is more than 2 inches thick at the thickest point, you can use an instant-read thermometer to check for doneness. The best type of thermometer to use is one with a digital display, because its temperature sensor is in the tip. Meat thermometers with a dial display have sensors farther up the stem and, therefore, are not as accurate with a thinner cut such as pork tenderloin.

When the pork tenderloin reaches 145°F, take it off the grill, loosely cover it with foil and let it rest for 10 minutes. The resting time allows juices from the surface to be reabsorbed into the meat. If you don't allow the meat to rest, the juices will run out when you cut the meat, and the meat will be dry.

Do a visual check for doneness for small pieces that can't be checked with a thermometer, such as skewered chunks of pork. Cook them until they are just slightly pink in the center.

PER SERVING: 250 calories, 14 g total fat (3 g saturated fat), 26.5 g protein, 5 g carbohydrate, 70 mg cholesterol, 380 mg sodium, 1 g fiber.

How to Stuff

To create a stuffed pork tenderloin, such as Peppered Pork Stuffed with Orange and Tarragon, first butterfly the pork. Spread the flattened meat with the stuffing, then roll up the meat lengthwise. Tie the roll with kitchen twine or insert several toothpicks or bamboo skewers to secure it before grilling.

internal temperature reaches 145°F, turning occasionally. Place pork on serving platter. Cover with foil; let stand 10 minutes.

4 Meanwhile, in small saucepan, stir together all sauce ingredients. Heat over medium heat until warm. (Sauce can be made up to 8 hours ahead. Cover and refrigerate. Reheat before use.)

5 To serve, slice pork diagonally. Serve with warm sauce.

6 servings.

Flavoring the Fire

The grill can do much more than simply cook pork tenderloin and other meats. Depending upon the type of coals used and extras added, grilling can actually be a seasoning "ingredient" in the recipe. Flavoring the fire is especially effective when grilling quick-cooking meat, such as pork tenderloin, as well as seafood and poultry.

The best charcoal is pure hardwood, but even good charcoal briquettes can be enhanced. The most common flavorings, and the most widely available, are wood chips. If you are using a gas grill, consult the owner's manual for directions for adding wood chips to

a smoker box. If your gas grill does not have a smoker box, wrap the chips in foil, punch holes in the packet with a pencil, and place the packet over one of the burners.

All flavoring agents provide more aromatic smoke if they are moist and tossed onto hot coals just before grilling. Wood chips and vines should be soaked 15 to 20 minutes. Fresh herbs and citrus peels can simply be spritzed with water.

Hickory chips They have an intense flavor and are best used with assertive marinades or tomato-based sauces.

Mesquite chips They lend a subtle smokiness best suited to recipes that use more delicate ingredients, such as herbs.

Aromatic chips Maple, cherry and apple, for example, work well with recipes using fruit and pork. Corncobs and citrus fruit peels add a distinctive aroma to the fire.

Vines Grapevines are especially good flavoring agents. And herb branches—sturdy ones such as rosemary—are also good.

Moroccan Lemon Chicken

Personal chefs share their clients' favorite do-ahead recipes.

Text by Carole Brown

There is one fantasy most cooks probably share—coming home to a delicious dinner that's been prepared by someone else. For some people, that dream has come true, thanks to the fast-growing field of personal chefs. A personal chef shops, cooks in your kitchen, cleans up and leaves the food in the fridge or freezer. Although they often cook sophisticated gourmet fare, their clients also request a fair share of down-home comfort food. Above all, these chefs specialize in making great do-ahead meals.

Unlike private chefs, personal chefs have many clients. And it's not only the well-heeled who hire them. Their typical clients are busy people who want good food, according to David MacKay, director of the United States Personal Chef Association (USPCA), a professional membership and training organization. Many of their clients love to cook, but their work and family schedules leave them with little time in the kitchen.

What kinds of foods do personal chefs prepare? We asked three USPCA members—Eric Gordon, Diane Lestina and Becky Trowbridge—to share some of their clients' favorite dishes. These oft-requested recipes are ideal for family dinners or casual entertaining, particularly because they can all be made ahead and refrigerated or frozen until you're ready to serve them. If you can't have personal chefs come to your home to prepare a meal, at least you can enjoy their recipes.

Moroccan Lemon Chicken

Diane Lestina's clients love her American food, but they often choose dishes that highlight her training in French, Italian, Cajun, Thai, Chinese and Lebanese cuisines. Warm Mediterranean spices highlight this dish. Serve it with cooked rice or couscous to absorb the fragrant broth. This recipe has been adapted from a U.S. Personal Chef Association recipe.

- 6 boneless skinless chicken breast halves
- ¼ teaspoon salt
- ⅛ teaspoon freshly ground pepper
- ¼ cup all-purpose flour
- 3 tablespoons olive oil
- 1 medium onion, thinly sliced
- 4 teaspoons grated lemon peel
- 1½ teaspoons ground cumin
- ½ teaspoon paprika
- ½ teaspoon cinnamon
- 2 cups reduced-sodium chicken broth
- 2 tablespoons lemon juice
- ⅔ cup pimiento-stuffed Spanish green olives
- 1 tablespoon honey
- ¼ cup chopped fresh cilantro
- 1 (15-oz.) can garbanzo beans, drained, rinsed

1 Sprinkle both sides of chicken breast halves with salt and pepper. Toss in flour; shake in strainer to remove excess flour.

2 Heat large skillet over medium-high heat until hot. Add 1 tablespoon of the olive oil; heat until hot. Add chicken in batches, if necessary; cook 6 minutes or until lightly browned, turning once, adding additional 1 tablespoon oil as needed.

Place chicken on plate.

3 Add remaining 1 tablespoon oil to skillet. Add onion; cook over medium-low heat 5 minutes or until soft and brown, stirring occasionally. Add lemon peel, cumin, paprika and cinnamon. Cook and stir 1 minute.

4 Stir in broth, lemon juice and olives. Return chicken and any accumulated juices to skillet. Bring to a boil over medium-high heat. Reduce heat to low; simmer 8 to 10 minutes or until no longer pink in center, turning chicken once. Stir in honey, cilantro and garbanzo beans. Cook 1 to 2 minutes or until garbanzo beans are thoroughly heated.

FREEZING/REHEATING Place chicken in freezer container. Pour remaining mixture over chicken; cool for 1 hour maximum. Cover and freeze. Twenty-four hours before serving, place container in refrigerator to thaw. Reheat on stove top or in microwave until thoroughly heated, stirring and turning chicken occasionally.

6 servings.

PER SERVING: 350 calories, 14 g total fat (2.5 g saturated fat), 33.5 g protein, 22.5 g carbohydrate, 65 mg cholesterol, 795 mg sodium, 3.5 g fiber.

Chicken Cacciatore

Full of hearty flavor and chunky vegetables, this dish, adapted from a U.S. Personal Chef Association recipe, is a natural to serve with rice or pasta. The recipe includes marinated artichoke hearts, but don't discard the marinade. Becky Trowbridge uses it to sauté the vegetables for an extra flavor boost.

CHICKEN
1½ lbs. boneless skinless chicken breast halves
¼ teaspoon salt
⅛ teaspoon freshly ground black pepper
¼ cup all-purpose flour
2 tablespoons olive oil

SAUCE
1 (6-oz.) jar marinated artichoke hearts, drained,

marinade reserved
2 cups sliced mushrooms
1 cup chopped onions
2 ribs celery, chopped
1 large carrot, chopped
½ red bell pepper, chopped
1 tablespoon minced garlic
1 (28-oz.) can diced tomatoes, undrained
1 (8-oz.) can tomato sauce
1½ tablespoons dried basil
1 tablespoon dried oregano
¾ teaspoon salt
⅛ teaspoon freshly ground black pepper
⅛ teaspoon crushed red pepper
3 medium bay leaves
½ cup (2 oz.) freshly grated Parmesan cheese

1 Heat oven to 350°F. Cut chicken into 1-inch pieces. Sprinkle with ¼ teaspoon salt and ⅛ teaspoon pepper. Toss chicken in flour; shake in strainer to remove excess flour.

2 Heat 1 tablespoon of the oil in large skillet over medium-high heat until hot. Cook chicken in batches 3 to 4 minutes or until browned, adding remaining 1 tablespoon oil as needed. Place chicken in 13x9-inch glass baking dish.

3 Add reserved artichoke marinade to skillet; heat over medium heat until hot, stirring to scrape up browned bits from bottom of skillet. Add mushrooms, onions, celery, carrot, bell pepper and garlic; cook 5 minutes or until vegetables begin to soften.

4 Add all remaining ingredients except cheese; mix well. Partially cover; simmer 10 minutes. Pour sauce over chicken. Cover with foil.

5 Bake 30 minutes or until hot and bubbly and chicken is no longer pink in center. Remove and discard bay leaves. Sprinkle with cheese.

FREEZING/REHEATING Remove dish from oven. Remove foil; cool for 1 hour maximum. Place in freezer container; cover and freeze. Parmesan cheese can be frozen in resealable plastic bag. Twenty-four hours before serving, place container in refrigerator to thaw. Reheat on

stove top or in microwave until thoroughly heated, stirring occasionally. Sprinkle with cheese.

8 servings.

PER SERVING: 235 calories, 8.5 g total fat (2.5 g saturated fat), 24 g protein, 16 g carbohydrate, 50 mg cholesterol, 825 mg sodium, 4 g fiber.

Spicy Black Bean and Sausage Soup

The distinctive smoky heat of chipotle chiles makes this hearty soup a winner with Eric Gordon's clients. Look for cans of chipotles in adobo sauce in the Mexican food section at your supermarket. Eric likes to use a spicy sausage, such as andouille or chorizo, in this soup, but you could use something milder, such as Polish sausage.

SOUP
2 tablespoons vegetable oil
½ lb. cooked chorizo sausage, sliced
1 large onion, coarsely chopped
1 red bell pepper, coarsely chopped
1 green bell pepper, coarsely chopped
3 garlic cloves, minced
1 to 2 chipotle chiles in adobo sauce, drained, chopped
2 tablespoons ground cumin
2 teaspoons ground coriander
1 teaspoon dried oregano
½ teaspoon sea salt
½ teaspoon freshly ground pepper
1 (14-oz.) can diced tomatoes with green chiles, undrained
2 cups reduced-sodium vegetable or chicken broth
2 (15-oz.) cans black beans, 1 can undrained and 1 can drained, rinsed
½ cup frozen corn

GARNISH
¼ cup chopped fresh cilantro
½ cup sliced green onions

Spicy Black Bean and Sausage Soup

1 Heat oil in large pot or Dutch oven over medium heat until hot. Add sausage; cook until browned. Remove from pot; place on plate.

2 Add onion, red bell pepper and green bell pepper; cook 2 to 3 minutes or until peppers begin to soften, stirring frequently. Cover; cook an additional 8 to 10 minutes or until vegetables are soft.

3 Add garlic, chipotle chiles, cumin, coriander, oregano, salt and pepper; cook briefly until spices are fragrant.

4 Stir in tomatoes, broth and undrained can of black beans; cover. Increase heat to medium-high; bring to a boil. Reduce heat to low; simmer 10 minutes.

5 Puree soup in batches in blender. Return soup to pot; add sausage, drained black beans and corn. Cook over medium heat until thoroughly heated, stirring occasionally. Garnish with cilantro and green onions.

FREEZING/REHEATING Place ungarnished soup in freezer container; cool for 1 hour maximum. Cover and freeze. Twenty-four hours before serving, place container in refrigerator to thaw. Reheat on stove top or in microwave until thoroughly heated, stirring occasionally. Garnish with cilantro and green onions.

6 (1½-cup) servings.

PER SERVING: 450 calories, 20.5 g total fat (6.5 g saturated fat), 21.5 g protein, 47 g carbohydrate, 35 mg cholesterol, 1205 mg sodium, 11 g fiber.

Kitchen Tips from the Chefs

Between them, Eric Gordon, Diane Lestina and Becky Trowbridge have prepared more than 36,000 meals for clients. They're constantly looking for ways to work more efficiently. These are some of their favorite tips.

Nonstick cooking spray

♦ When using sticky ingredients, such as peanut butter or honey, spray measuring cups and spoons with a thin coat of nonstick cooking spray to make cleanup easier.

♦ Lightly coat the food processor bowl with nonstick cooking spray before adding ingredients to make them easier to remove.

♦ To prevent a tomato dish from leaving orange stains in plastic containers, spray the container with nonstick cooking spray.

Helpful tools

♦ Use an immersion blender to puree soup or sauce right in the cooking pot.

♦ Use a salad spinner to rinse and dry fresh herbs. It works quickly and removes most of the moisture for easy chopping.

♦ A flexible cutting mat is great for preparing raw meat, poultry and fish. It keeps them isolated from other foods. When you're done, set the mat aside for cleaning, and switch to another mat or cutting board to prepare other ingredients.

Cooking tips

♦ After dredging pieces of meat in flour, toss them in a strainer over the sink to remove excess flour before sautéing. This leaves a light, thin coating of flour that doesn't get cakey.

♦ To avoid dry meat and mushy pasta, slightly undercook them in dishes prepared in advance. They will finish cooking when you reheat the dish.

♦ For a refreshing flavor boost to a recipe that uses fresh herbs, reserve some of the herbs and add them during the last few minutes of cooking or when reheating the dish.

Rosemary Beef Stew

"Liquid gold" is how one of Diane Lestina's clients labeled this dish. She suggests serving it with mashed potatoes. This recipe has been adapted from a U.S. Personal Chef Association recipe.

- 1/3 cup all-purpose flour
- 3/4 teaspoon salt
- 1/4 teaspoon plus 1/8 teaspoon freshly ground pepper
- 2 lbs. beef round or chuck steak, cut into 3/4-inch pieces
- 2 to 3 tablespoons olive oil
- 1/2 cup dry red wine
- 2 (14.5-oz.) cans diced tomatoes, undrained
- 2 ribs celery, thinly sliced diagonally
- 2 garlic cloves, minced
- 1/2 cup coarsely chopped fresh parsley
- 1/2 teaspoon dried basil
- 1/4 teaspoon dried oregano
- 1/4 teaspoon dried thyme
- 1 1/2 tablespoons chopped fresh rosemary
- 8 oz. mushrooms, sliced
- 2 medium fennel bulbs, fronds removed, cut into thin wedges
- 2 1/2 to 3 cups beef broth
- 1 cup frozen small whole white onions

1 In shallow pan, mix together flour, 1/4 teaspoon of the salt and 1/8 teaspoon of the pepper. Pat beef dry with paper towels. Toss in flour mixture to coat thoroughly; shake in strainer to remove excess flour.

2 Heat nonreactive Dutch oven over medium-high heat until hot. Add 1 tablespoon of the oil. Cook beef in batches 4 to 6 minutes or until browned, adding additional oil as needed. Place beef in bowl.

3 Increase heat to high. Add wine; bring to a boil. Boil until reduced by half, stirring to scrape up browned bits from bottom of Dutch oven.

4 Stir in tomatoes, celery, garlic, parsley, basil, oregano, thyme, remaining 1/2 teaspoon salt and 1/4 teaspoon pepper, and 1 tablespoon of the rosemary. Stir in mushrooms, fennel and beef. Add enough broth to cover mixture.

5 Cover; simmer 45 minutes. Add onions; continue simmering 30 to 45 minutes or until beef is tender.

6 Stir in remaining 1/2 tablespoon chopped rosemary; simmer an additional 10 minutes.

FREEZING/REHEATING Place stew in freezer container; cool for 1 hour maximum. Cover and freeze. Twenty-four hours before serving, place container in refrigerator to thaw. Reheat on stove top or in microwave until thoroughly heated, stirring occasionally.

8 servings.

PER SERVING: 235 calories, 7.5 g total fat (1.5 g saturated fat), 27.5 g protein, 15 g carbohydrate, 60 mg cholesterol, 760 mg sodium, 3.5 g fiber.

Freezing & Storing

All of the recipes here can be assembled, cooked and then frozen for up to six months. To make certain the food keeps well during freezing and storing, follow these suggestions.

♦ Cool or chill foods before covering and freezing them. If moisture from warm food condenses inside the container it's stored in, ice forms and makes the food watery when it thaws.

♦ Freezer burn occurs when food is exposed to air and becomes dry. To avoid it, package food in freezer bags or containers that keep out moisture, air and odors. Another way to discourage freezer burn is to put plastic wrap directly on top of the food after filling a container. Then put on the cover. Remember to remove the plastic wrap before reheating. You can also double-bag food.

♦ Using a permanent marker, write the date and contents directly on the package or on freezer tape.

Lasagna
Revival

Mediterranean Vegetable Lasagna

An old friend gets reinvented with fresh flavor combinations.

Recipes by Carole Brown

If Americans were asked to vote for their favorite comfort food, lasagna just might be the winner. When you consider lasagna's basic ingredients—pasta, meat, cheese and sauce—and the fact that it's a one-dish meal, it's easy to understand its popularity.

But being popular is a two-edged sword. When you're commonplace, you risk being labeled ordinary and boring. So how do you get noticed again? Reinvent yourself. Take on a new ingredient or two. Change your sauce. Add some spice. All of a sudden, you've earned a spot in the limelight again.

These lasagnas are every bit the comfort food of their traditional counterparts. And they'll still elicit "mmms" and "ahhs." And call your friends. These reinvented dishes are worthy of a party.

Mediterranean Vegetable Lasagna

This lasagna is full of sunny Mediterranean flavors. The sheep's milk Pecorino Romano cheese adds a nice tangy and salty flavor, but you can substitute regular Romano or Parmesan cheese.

LASAGNA
12 lasagna noodles

FILLING
1 medium eggplant, unpeeled, cut into ½-inch pieces
6 tablespoons olive oil
1 cup finely chopped onions
1 green bell pepper, finely chopped
2 garlic cloves, minced
½ teaspoon salt
¼ teaspoon freshly ground black pepper
⅛ teaspoon crushed red pepper
2 tablespoons red wine vinegar
1½ cups canned crushed tomatoes in puree
1 cup pitted Kalamata olives, sliced
1 (15-oz.) can garbanzo beans, drained, rinsed
½ cup chopped fresh basil

SAUCE
3 cups ricotta cheese (about 2 lbs.)
½ cup milk
1½ cups (6 oz.) grated Pecorino Romano cheese
1 cup chopped fresh Italian parsley
2 tablespoons grated lemon peel
2 teaspoons dried mint
½ teaspoon salt
¼ teaspoon freshly ground black pepper

Salmon Lasagna with Creamy Basil Sauce

1 Heat oven to 425°F. Cook lasagna noodles according to package directions. Rinse under cold running water to cool; drain. In large bowl, toss eggplant with 3 tablespoons of the oil; spread on large rimmed baking sheet. Bake 15 to 20 minutes or until tender and lightly browned, stirring once. Remove from oven; reduce oven temperature to 375°F.

2 Meanwhile, heat remaining 3 tablespoons oil in large skillet over medium heat until hot. Add onions and bell pepper; cook 5 to 8 minutes or until softened. Add garlic, ½ teaspoon salt, ¼ teaspoon black pepper and red pepper; cook 2 to 3 minutes or until garlic is soft. Add vinegar; cook and stir until vinegar has evaporated. Stir in tomatoes; simmer 10 minutes or until slightly thickened. Remove from heat. Gently stir in olives, garbanzo beans, basil and eggplant.

3 In large bowl, whisk together ricotta cheese and milk until smooth. Reserve ⅓ cup cheese. Add remaining cheese, parsley, lemon peel, mint, ½ teaspoon salt and ¼ teaspoon black pepper to ricotta cheese mixture; mix well.

4 Grease 13x9-inch pan. Arrange 3 lasagna noodles in pan, overlapping or trimming as necessary. Spread noodles with half of the filling. Top with 3 noodles; spread with half of the cheese sauce. Repeat layers. Sprinkle with reserved Pecorino Romano cheese. Cover with foil.

5 Bake at 375°F for 45 to 50 minutes or until lasagna is hot throughout. Remove foil; bake an additional 10 minutes. Let stand 15 minutes.

12 servings.

PER SERVING: 365 calories, 18 g total fat (7 g saturated fat), 18.5 g protein, 34 g carbohydrate, 30 mg cholesterol, 830 mg sodium, 4.5 g fiber.

Salmon Lasagna with Creamy Basil Sauce

This elegant lasagna is ideal for a small dinner party. Slightly undercook the salmon because it will finish cooking when it is baked in the lasagna. All the elements of this lasagna can be prepared in advance and refrigerated until you are ready to cook the pasta and assemble the lasagna. Or the whole lasagna can be made ahead and refrigerated.

LASAGNA
12 lasagna noodles
1½ cups (6 oz.) grated
    Parmesan cheese

SALMON
4 cups water
½ lemon, coarsely chopped
1 (1½-lbs.) salmon fillet, skin on

SAUCE
2 tablespoons unsalted butter
3 tablespoons all-purpose flour
1½ cups milk
1½ cups whipping cream
½ teaspoon salt
¼ teaspoon freshly ground pepper
⅔ cup chopped fresh basil or
    2 tablespoons prepared
    pesto

FILLING
2 tablespoons extra-virgin
    olive oil
1 cup finely chopped onions
2 garlic cloves, minced
1 teaspoon dried thyme
¼ teaspoon salt
¼ teaspoon freshly ground pepper
4 cups grated zucchini
3 tablespoons chopped fresh
    Italian parsley

1 Cook lasagna noodles according to package directions. Rinse under cold running water to cool; drain. Meanwhile, cook salmon. In large skillet, combine water and lemon. Bring to a boil over medium heat. Add salmon; cover and reduce heat to medium-low. Simmer 5 to 8 minutes or until outside edge of salmon is opaque. Drain on paper towels. Remove skin; flake salmon into pieces. Cover and refrigerate. Discard broth.

2 Melt butter in medium saucepan over medium heat. Whisk in flour; cook 1 minute, whisking constantly. Do not let flour brown. Whisk in milk, cream, ½ teaspoon salt and ¼ teaspoon pepper. Bring to a boil, whisking constantly. Reduce heat to low; simmer 10 minutes, stirring occasionally.

3 Add basil; simmer an additional 5 minutes. Cool slightly. (Sauce can be made up to 1 day ahead. Place plastic wrap directly on surface of sauce to keep skin from forming; refrigerate.)

4 Heat oil in large skillet over medium heat until hot. Add onions; cook 3 to 5 minutes or until soft but not browned. Stir in garlic, thyme, ¼ teaspoon salt and ¼ teaspoon pepper. Cook 1 to 2 minutes or until garlic is soft. Stir in zucchini. Increase heat to medium-high; cook 5 to 8 minutes or until zucchini is tender and liquid has evaporated, stirring frequently. Adjust heat if necessary. Stir in parsley.

5 Heat oven to 375°F. Grease 8-inch square pan. Reserve ½ cup of the sauce and ½ cup of the Parmesan cheese. Arrange 3 noodles in pan, overlapping or trimming as necessary. Spread noodles with one-third each of the remaining sauce, salmon, filling and remaining Parmesan cheese. Repeat layers twice. Top with remaining 3 noodles, reserved sauce and Parmesan cheese.

6 Bake, uncovered, 35 to 40 minutes or until lasagna is hot throughout. Let stand 15 minutes.

6 servings.

PER SERVING: 730 calories, 42 g total fat (22 g saturated fat), 41.5 g protein, 46 g carbohydrate, 165 mg cholesterol, 1025 mg sodium, 3.5 g fiber.

Italian Sausage and Broccoli Lasagna with Creamy Tomato Sauce

This lasagna has it all—bold, zingy flavors and a luxurious touch of cream in the tomato sauce. The quality of the Italian sausage is very important to the success of this recipe. Search out good sausage that is full of flavor and not too fatty. Because of the cream in the tomato sauce, the recipe doesn't need a lot of cheese.

LASAGNA
12 lasagna noodles

3 cups broccoli florets
1½ lbs. bulk mild Italian sausage
1 (7- to 8-oz.) jar roasted red bell peppers, drained, chopped
2 cups (8 oz.) shredded mozzarella cheese

SAUCE
2 tablespoons extra-virgin olive oil
2 cups finely chopped onions
6 garlic cloves, minced
2 teaspoons dried oregano
½ teaspoon crushed red pepper
¼ teaspoon salt
¼ teaspoon freshly ground black pepper
1 (28-oz.) can crushed tomatoes in puree
1½ cups sour cream
½ cup chopped fresh Italian parsley

1 Cook lasagna noodles according to package directions. Rinse under cold running water to cool; drain. Meanwhile, to make sauce, heat olive oil in large saucepan over medium heat until hot. Add onions; cook 3 to 5 minutes or until soft but not browned. Add garlic, oregano, red pepper, salt and black pepper; cook 2 to 3 minutes or until garlic is soft but not browned. Add tomatoes; simmer 10 minutes, stirring occasionally. Remove from heat; cool slightly. Stir in sour cream and parsley.

2 Cook broccoli in large saucepan of boiling salted water 4 minutes or until partially cooked. Rinse under cold running water to cool.

3 Cook sausage in large skillet over medium-high heat in batches, if necessary, until no longer pink, stirring frequently. Remove sausage from pan; drain on paper towels.

4 In large bowl, stir together sausage and bell peppers.

5 Heat oven to 375°F. Grease 13x9-inch pan. Reserve 1 cup of the sauce and 1 cup of the cheese. Arrange 3 lasagna noodles in pan, overlapping or trimming as necessary. Spread noodles with one-third each of the remaining sauce, sausage, broccoli and remaining cheese.

Repeat layers twice. Top with remaining 3 noodles, reserved sauce and cheese. Cover with foil.

6 Bake 40 to 45 minutes or until lasagna is hot and bubbly. Remove foil; bake an additional 10 minutes. Let stand 15 minutes.

12 servings.

PER SERVING: 335 calories, 19 g total fat (8.5 g saturated fat), 16 g protein, 25.5 g carbohydrate, 50 mg cholesterol, 645 mg sodium, 3 g fiber.

Wild Mushroom Lasagna with Pancetta and Fontina Cheese

The robust flavor of dried Italian porcini mushrooms (also known as cepes) makes this an ideal dish for a fall dinner or buffet. Porcini and pancetta, unsmoked Italian bacon, are sold in many supermarkets and specialty food shops. If you can't find porcini, leave them out and make the mushroom sauce with 4 cups of milk.

LASAGNA
12 lasagna noodles
3 cups (12 oz.) shredded fontina cheese
1½ cups (6 oz.) grated Parmesan cheese

SAUCE
1 oz. dried porcini mushrooms
2 cups boiling water
2 tablespoons olive oil
⅓ cup (2 oz.) chopped pancetta
1 cup chopped onions
12 oz. button or crimini mushrooms, sliced
2 garlic cloves, minced
1½ teaspoons dried sage
1 teaspoon salt
½ teaspoon freshly ground pepper
⅛ teaspoon cayenne pepper
¼ cup brandy or porcini soaking liquid
¼ cup all-purpose flour
3 cups milk
½ cup chopped fresh Italian parsley

1 Cook lasagna noodles according to package directions. Rinse under cold running water to cool; drain.

Meanwhile, in medium bowl, soak porcini mushrooms in boiling water 15 to 20 minutes or until mushrooms are soft. Drain, reserving liquid. Strain liquid through coffee filter or cheesecloth to remove any particles. Coarsely chop mushrooms.

2 Heat oil in large pot or Dutch oven over medium heat until hot. Add pancetta; cook 2 to 4 minutes or until pancetta is lightly browned. Add onions; cook 3 to 5 minutes or until soft. Increase heat to medium-high. Add button mushrooms; cook 3 to 5 minutes or until liquid has evaporated and mushrooms are lightly browned, stirring occasionally. Stir in garlic, sage, salt, pepper, cayenne pepper and porcini mushrooms. Add brandy; cook until liquid has evaporated.

3 Reduce heat to medium-low. Stir flour into mushroom mixture. Cook and stir 1 minute. Add milk and 1 cup of the reserved porcini soaking liquid. Bring to a boil over medium heat, stirring occasionally. Reduce heat to low; simmer 10 minutes, stirring occasionally and scraping up browned bits from bottom of pot. Stir in parsley.

4 Heat oven to 375°F. Grease 13x9-inch pan. In medium bowl, combine fontina and Parmesan cheeses. Reserve 1 cup of the cheese mixture and 1 cup of the sauce. Arrange 3 lasagna noodles in pan, overlapping or trimming as necessary. Spread noodles with one-third each of the remaining sauce and cheese mixture. Repeat layers twice. Top with remaining 3 noodles, reserved sauce and cheese mixture. Cover with foil.

5 Bake 40 to 45 minutes or until lasagna is hot throughout. Remove foil; bake an additional 10 minutes. Let stand 15 minutes.

12 servings.

PER SERVING: 370 calories, 21 g total fat (11 g saturated fat), 19 g protein, 24.5 g carbohydrate, 45 mg cholesterol, 770 mg sodium, 1.5 g fiber.

Noodle News

What's the best way to hold lasagna noodles after they've been cooked but before the lasagna is assembled? To prevent them from sticking to one another, spread them out on a baking sheet that's been lined with parchment paper, making sure the noodles don't overlap.

Sweet Highlights

Desserts and treats impossible to resist.

Swedish Almond-Cardamom Biscotti.
Cranberry-Ginger Shortbread.

Simplify holiday baking with festive bar cookies.

Text and Recipes by Beatrice Ojakangas

There was a time when I went overboard baking fancy holiday cookies. I'd make a different recipe every day for weeks before Christmas, taking pains to make certain the cookies were as beautiful as they were delicious. They were used for gifts and, of course, served as desserts.

These days, it seems there is far less time for baking, but you still can make cookies to give and serve over the holidays. Just supplement your favorite traditional recipes with bar cookies. Although you can't make fancy cutout shapes with bars, you can make confections in geometrical shapes—diamonds, rectangles, triangles and squares. With far less effort, they're every bit as tasty and pretty.

Swedish Almond-Cardamom Biscotti

A richly flavored cookie dough is baked in a 15x10x1-inch pan, then sliced and toasted until crisp and crunchy. The biscotti are delicious plain or dipped into melted chocolate for a special holiday touch.

- 3½ cups all-purpose flour
- ½ cup finely chopped unblanched almonds
- 1 tablespoon ground cardamom*
- 2 teaspoons baking powder
- ½ teaspoon salt
- 1 cup unsalted butter, softened
- 2 cups sugar
- 1 (8-oz.) container sour cream
- 2 eggs
- 16 oz. semisweet chocolate, chopped

1 Heat oven to 350°F. Lightly spray 15x10x1-inch pan with nonstick cooking spray.

2 In medium bowl, stir together flour, almonds, cardamom, baking powder and salt. In large bowl, beat butter and sugar at medium speed until smooth. Add sour cream and eggs; beat 1 to 2 minutes or until light and fluffy. At low speed, add flour mixture, beating just until smooth. Spread dough evenly in pan.

3 Bake 25 to 30 minutes or until top is light golden brown. Remove from oven; cool on wire rack 10 minutes. Reduce oven temperature to 325°F.

4 Cut biscotti in half lengthwise; cut each strip crosswise into ½-inch slices. Place slices close together, cut side up, in single layer on baking sheet.

Honey-Cashew Confections
Marbled Cinnamon Marzipan Brownies

5 Bake 40 minutes or until dry and crisp, turning once. Place baking sheet with cookies on wire rack to cool.

6 Place chocolate in medium bowl. Place over very hot water; let stand until melted, stirring occasionally. Dip ends of biscotti diagonally in chocolate; place on sheet of foil. Let stand until chocolate is set. Store in airtight container.

TIP *For the best flavor, remove cardamom seeds from the pods and grind them just before using. Purchased ground cardamom has lost some of its flavor by the time you get it into your kitchen.

About 60 cookies.

PER COOKIE: 130 calories, 7 g total fat (4 g saturated fat), 1.5 g protein, 17.5 g carbohydrate, 20 mg cholesterol, 40 mg sodium, 1 g fiber.

Honey-Cashew Confections

Plenty of cashews top this candy-like nut-lover's bar.

CRUST
- 1½ cups all-purpose flour
- ½ cup packed brown sugar
- ¼ teaspoon salt
- ½ cup unsalted butter, chilled, cut up

TOPPING
- 1 cup packed brown sugar
- ½ cup unsalted butter
- ¼ cup honey
- ¼ teaspoon cream of tartar
- 2 cups whole salted cashews

1 Heat oven to 350°F. Spray 13x9-inch pan with nonstick cooking spray. Combine flour, ½ cup brown sugar and salt in food processor; pulse until blended. Add ½ cup butter; pulse until mixture resembles coarse crumbs. Press crumb mixture in bottom of pan. Bake 10 to 12 minutes or until light brown.

2 Meanwhile, combine 1 cup brown

sugar, ½ cup butter and honey in medium saucepan; cook over medium-low heat 6 to 7 minutes or until mixture comes to a boil, stirring frequently. Remove from heat. Add cream of tartar; mix well.

3 Spread cashews evenly over crust. Pour brown sugar mixture evenly over nuts. Return to oven; bake an additional 10 to 12 minutes or until bubbly and lightly browned. Cool in pan on wire rack 20 to 25 minutes. Cut into bars while still warm. Cool completely.

48 bars.

PER BAR: 110 calories, 12.5 g total fat (6.5 g saturated fat), 1.5 g protein, 12.5 g carbohydrate, 10 mg cholesterol, 7.5 mg sodium, .5 g fiber.

Marbled Cinnamon Marzipan Brownies

The marzipan filling swirled into the rich chocolate batter makes a pretty design on these brownies.

BROWNIES
- 1 cup unsalted butter
- 4 oz. unsweetened chocolate, chopped
- 2 cups sugar
- 1 teaspoon cinnamon
- 2 teaspoons vanilla
- 4 eggs
- 1 cup all-purpose flour

FILLING
- 1 (7- to 8-oz.) pkg. almond paste
- ¼ teaspoon cinnamon
- 1 egg

1 Heat oven to 350°F. Spray 13x9-inch pan with nonstick cooking spray. Melt butter in medium saucepan over low heat. Add chocolate; cook and stir 1 to 2 minutes or until melted. Remove from heat. Stir in sugar, 1 teaspoon cinnamon and vanilla. Add 4 eggs, one at a time, beating well after each addition. Add flour; mix until smooth. Spread batter evenly in pan.

2 Crumble almond paste into food processor. Process until finely chopped. Add ¼ teaspoon cinnamon and 1 egg; process until completely smooth. Drop almond mixture by small spoonfuls onto brownie batter. Swirl with knife.

3 Bake 30 to 35 minutes or until toothpick inserted in center comes out almost clean.

48 bars.

PER BAR: 120 calories, 7 g total fat (3.5 g saturated fat), 1.5 g protein, 14 g carbohydrate, 30 mg cholesterol, 10 mg sodium, .5 g fiber.

Apricot Streusel Bars

The buttery walnut crust and streusel topping encase a tangy apricot filling.

FILLING
- 1 (6-oz.) pkg. dried apricots (about 1 cup)
- 1 cup water
- 4 eggs
- 3 tablespoons fresh lemon juice
- 1½ cups sugar

Apricot Streusel Bars

Raspberry Diamonds

⅓ cup all-purpose flour
½ teaspoon salt

CRUST
2 cups all-purpose flour
1 cup coarsely chopped walnuts
¾ cup powdered sugar
1 cup unsalted butter, chilled,
     cut up

GARNISH
Powdered sugar

1 Heat oven to 350°F. Spray 13x9-inch pan with nonstick cooking spray. In medium saucepan, combine apricots and water; simmer, uncovered, over medium-low to low heat 25 minutes or until liquid is absorbed, stirring occasionally. Cool.

2 Meanwhile, place 2 cups flour, walnuts and ¾ cup powdered sugar in food processor; process until blended and nuts are finely chopped. Add butter; process until mixture resembles coarse crumbs (do not process until mixture becomes smooth). Reserve 1½ cups crumb mixture. Press remaining mixture in

bottom of pan.

3 Bake 12 to 15 minutes or until lightly browned around edges.

4 Meanwhile, place cooked apricots in same food processor (no need to wash first). Add eggs, lemon juice, sugar, ⅓ cup flour and salt; process until blended.

5 Pour filling over crust. Sprinkle with reserved 1½ cups crumb mixture. Return to oven; bake an additional 25 to 30 minutes or until filling is set and top is light brown. Cool in pan on wire rack. Cut into bars. Sprinkle with powdered sugar.

48 bars.

PER BAR: 120 calories, 6 g total fat (2.5 g saturated fat), 1.5 g protein, 15.5 g carbohydrate, 30 mg cholesterol, 30 mg sodium, .5 g fiber.

Raspberry Diamonds

Coffee and cocoa team up to create a mocha-flavored bar that's topped with raspberry preserves and a drizzle of frosting.

BARS
1 cup unsalted butter, softened
½ cup sugar
½ cup packed brown sugar
2 tablespoons instant coffee
½ teaspoon baking soda
½ teaspoon salt
1 teaspoon vanilla
1 egg yolk
2½ cups all-purpose flour
1 teaspoon unsweetened cocoa
¾ cup raspberry preserves

FROSTING
¾ cup powdered sugar
1 tablespoon unsalted butter,
     softened
1 to 2 tablespoons milk

1 In large bowl, combine 1 cup butter, sugar and brown sugar; beat at medium speed until well blended. Add coffee, baking soda, salt, vanilla and egg yolk; beat until well mixed.

2 In medium bowl, stir together flour and cocoa. At low speed, add flour mixture to butter mixture, mixing until stiff dough forms. Shape dough into flattened rectangle; cover with

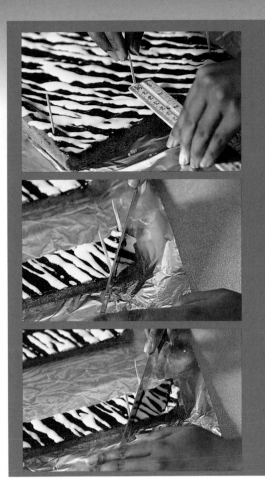

Clean Cuts

Here's how to cut picture-perfect Raspberry Diamond bars.

Cut the bars on a counter It's easier to cut bar cookies if you remove them from the pan first. To do so, line the pan with foil, leaving enough at the ends to act as handles. After baking, cool the recipe completely in the pan; then lift out the uncut bars with the foil.

Measure and mark cuts Trim uneven edges, if desired. Using a ruler and toothpicks, measure and mark the location of your cuts. For the diamond shape, cut the bars in 1¼-inch-wide strips. Then mark the four points of the diamond: Start at one corner of the strip and mark 1½ inches down that edge. On the opposite edge, mark ¾ inch from the corner; then mark 1½ inches from that point. Make the angled cuts as marked, using the toothpicks as your guide. To cut the remaining diamond shapes, simply measure 1½ inches from the previous cut. Repeat this procedure for each strip.

Use the proper knife Cut bars with a sharp, straight-edged knife. Be sure to dip the knife in hot water after each cut and then wipe it off.

plastic wrap. Refrigerate at least 1 hour or up to 2 days.

3 Heat oven to 350°F. Press chilled dough in bottom of ungreased 13x9-inch pan. Bake 15 to 18 minutes or until set and light brown.

4 Meanwhile, in medium bowl, combine all frosting ingredients; blend until smooth.

5 Remove bars from oven. Immediately spread with raspberry preserves. Drizzle with frosting. Cool in pan on wire rack. Cut into diamond-shaped bars.

About 45 bars.

PER BAR: 105 calories, 4.5 g total fat (3 g saturated fat), 1 g protein, 15.5 g carbohydrate, 15 mg cholesterol, 45 mg sodium, .5 g fiber.

Cranberry-Ginger Shortbread

The sweet-hot tang of ginger and chewy tartness of dried cranberries makes these shortbread wedges irresistible. A tree trunk made with a halved pecan and a drizzle of frosting turn the wedges into Christmas trees.

SHORTBREAD
- 2¼ cups all-purpose flour
- ½ cup sugar
- ¼ teaspoon salt
- 1 cup unsalted butter, chilled, cut up
- 1 teaspoon grated fresh ginger
- ¼ cup finely chopped crystallized ginger
- 1 cup dried cranberries
- 24 pecan halves
- 2 teaspoons sugar

GLAZE
- ¾ cup powdered sugar
- ¾ teaspoon grated fresh ginger
- 2 to 3 teaspoons milk

1 Heat oven to 300°F. Line baking sheet with parchment paper; using 8-inch round cake pan as a guide, draw 2 (8-inch) circles about 1 inch apart on paper.

2 In food processor, combine flour, ½ cup sugar and salt; pulse until blended. Add butter; pulse until mixture resembles moist sand. Add 1 teaspoon fresh ginger; continue processing until smooth dough forms. Place dough on lightly floured surface. Add crystallized ginger and cranberries; knead until evenly distributed.

3 Divide dough in half; shape each half into flattened round. Place 1 round in center of each circle on parchment paper. Flatten dough to within ½ inch of circle.

4 Cut each round into 12 wedges; do not separate. Press pecan half on bottom edge of each wedge to resemble trunk of Christmas tree. Sprinkle each round with 1 teaspoon sugar.

5 Bake 1 hour or until shortbread is lightly browned. Immediately cut to separate wedges. Remove from baking sheet; cool on wire racks.

6 Meanwhile, combine powdered sugar, ¾ teaspoon fresh ginger and enough milk to make a thin glaze. Drizzle glaze over wedges to resemble tinsel on trees.

24 bars.

PER BAR: 170 calories, 8.5 g total fat (5 g saturated fat), 1.5 g protein, 23 g carbohydrate, 20 mg cholesterol, 30 mg sodium, .5 g fiber.

Cocoa
Heaven

Cocoa-Pecan Roulade

These divine confections get their chocolaty richness from an earthly ingredient—cocoa powder.

Text and Recipes by Alice Medrich

In my house "dessert" means "chocolate." The basic ingredients are always on hand: chocolate baking bars, sugar, flour … and two kinds of cocoa.

Cocoa is the essence of chocolate in a dry, concentrated form. It has an extremely potent flavor because some of the fat has been removed. Cocoa is often superior to unsweetened baking chocolate in cakes and cookies because it delivers an intense chocolate flavor along with a tender crumb and light texture—a combination of qualities that's hard to achieve with solid baking chocolate. What's more, cocoa is easy to measure and mix, it requires no melting and it keeps well.

If you've neglected cocoa for the hard stuff, take another look. Cocoa is a versatile secret weapon in a dessert-maker's arsenal.

Cocoa-Pecan Roulade

The texture of this exceptionally fudgy cake is different from the typical rolled cake: It's very moist and tender rather than dry and airy. You should expect to see cracks when you roll it.

CAKE
- ½ cup pecan halves
- 2 tablespoons all-purpose flour
- 1 cup sugar
- ½ cup unsweetened Dutch-process cocoa
- ⅛ teaspoon salt
- ¾ cup unsalted butter
- 4 eggs, separated
- 1 teaspoon vanilla
- ⅛ teaspoon cream of tartar

FILLING
- 1 cup heavy whipping cream
- 2 teaspoons instant espresso coffee powder
- ½ teaspoon vanilla
- 2 tablespoons sugar

GARNISH
Cocoa
Powdered sugar

1 Heat oven to 350°F. Spread pecans in 17x12x1-inch pan. Bake 5 to 8 minutes or until fragrant and lightly colored. Place pecans on plate to cool. Spray bottom of same pan with nonstick cooking spray; line with parchment paper. Spray pan and paper with nonstick cooking spray; lightly flour.

2 In food processor, combine pecans and flour; pulse until nuts are finely ground.

3 In large bowl, stir with whisk ¾ cup of the sugar, cocoa and salt; mix well. In small saucepan over medium heat, melt butter. Whisk butter into cocoa mixture. Whisk in egg yolks and vanilla.

4 In another large bowl, beat egg whites and cream of tartar at medium speed until soft peaks form. Gradually add remaining ¼ cup sugar, beating at high speed until stiff but not dry. Fold ¼ of beaten egg whites into cocoa mixture. Add remaining egg whites and pecan mixture to batter; fold just until incorporated. Spread batter evenly in pan.

5 Bake 10 to 12 minutes or until cake is puffy, moist and toothpick inserted in center comes out almost clean (a few crumbs will remain). Do not overbake. Cool in pan on wire rack.

6 Sift a light dusting of cocoa over 18-inch square sheet of foil. Invert cake onto foil; peel off parchment paper.

7 In large bowl, beat cream, coffee powder and ½ teaspoon vanilla at medium-high speed until mixture begins to thicken. Sprinkle 2 tablespoons sugar over cream; beat until soft peaks form. Spread cream over cake. Starting with long side, roll cake using foil as guide.* (Cake will crack as it is rolled, but cracks will become less severe as cake roll gets larger. Cake will have a craggy, bark-like appearance.) Cover; refrigerate until serving time.

8 To serve, place on platter. Sprinkle with cocoa and powdered sugar. Store in refrigerator.

TIP *For a shorter, wider cake, roll cake starting with short side.

12 servings.

PER SERVING: 310 calories, 23.5 g total fat (12 g saturated fat), 4 g protein, 24.5 g carbohydrate, 125 mg cholesterol, 55 mg sodium, 2 g fiber.

Bittersweet Cocoa Soufflés

These terrifically simple soufflés can be prepared in advance, except for the baking. To serve, simply put them into a hot oven for 12 to 16 minutes while you clear the table. Dutch-process or natural cocoa is appropriate here.

SOUFFLÉS
- ½ cup unsalted butter
- ⅔ cup unsweetened cocoa
- ½ cup plus 3 tablespoons sugar
- 1 tablespoon all-purpose flour
- ¼ teaspoon salt
- ⅓ cup milk
- 3 egg yolks, room temperature
- 1 teaspoon vanilla
- 4 egg whites, room temperature
- ⅛ teaspoon cream of tartar
- 2 tablespoons powdered sugar

GARNISH
- 1 cup whipping cream
- 2 teaspoons sugar
- 1 teaspoon vanilla

1 Grease 8 (6-oz.) soufflé dishes or ramekins with butter; lightly sprinkle with sugar. Melt butter in small saucepan over medium heat. Add cocoa, ½ cup of the sugar, flour, salt and milk; mix well. Cook until

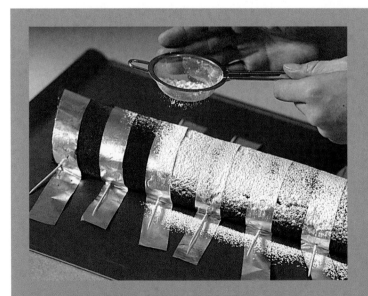

Decorating Roulade

To decorate the Cocoa-Pecan Roulade with stripes, cut foil into 1-inch-wide pieces. Place the strips on the assembled roulade as shown, leaving 1-inch gaps between strips. Secure the strips with toothpicks and sift powdered sugar over the cake. Reposition the strips over the powdered sugar strips and sift unsweetened Dutch-process cocoa over the cake.

Crumb Coat

For a crumb-free frosting on the Cocoa Génoise and other cakes, use the crumb coat technique. Brush loose crumbs from the cake, then apply a thin coat of frosting. Don't worry about crumbs that may appear. Put the cake in the refrigerator for 15 to 30 minutes to slightly harden the frosting. Then finish frosting the cake.

Cocoa Génoise with Crème Fraîche and Raspberries

mixture is smooth and small bubbles begin to form around edges, stirring constantly. Pour mixture into large bowl. Whisk in egg yolks and 1 teaspoon vanilla.

2 In large bowl, beat egg whites and cream of tartar at medium speed until soft peaks form. Gradually add remaining 3 tablespoons sugar, beating at high speed until egg whites are stiff but not dry. Fold ¼ of egg whites into cocoa mixture; fold in remaining egg whites.

3 Divide batter evenly into cups. Place cups on baking sheet. (Soufflés can be prepared up to 24 hours ahead. Cover and refrigerate.)

4 When ready to bake soufflés, heat oven to 375°F. In small bowl, beat cream, 2 teaspoons sugar and 1 teaspoon vanilla at medium-high speed until soft peaks form. Refrigerate until ready to serve.

5 Bake soufflés on baking sheet 12 to 16 minutes or until soufflés are puffed, cracked and toothpick inserted in center comes out slightly moist

but not wet. Remove from oven; sift powdered sugar over tops. Serve immediately with whipped cream.

8 servings.

PER SERVING: 325 calories, 26.5 g total fat (24 g saturated fat), 5.5 g protein, 24 g carbohydrate, 145 mg cholesterol, 120 mg sodium, 2.5 g fiber.

Cocoa Génoise with Crème Fraîche and Raspberries

CAKE
- ⅓ cup plus 1 tablespoon sifted all-purpose flour
- ⅓ cup plus 1 tablespoon sifted unsweetened Dutch-process cocoa
- 4 eggs
- ⅔ cup sugar
- 3 tablespoons clarified unsalted butter, warm*
- 1 teaspoon vanilla

FILLING AND FROSTING
- 2 cups crème fraîche**

- 1 cup whipping cream
- 2 tablespoons sugar
- 1½ teaspoons vanilla
- ½ cup Chambord liqueur or raspberry juice blend
- 3 cups fresh raspberries

1 Heat oven to 350°F. Line bottom of 9x1½-inch round pan with parchment paper. Spray parchment paper with nonstick cooking spray; sprinkle with flour. (Leave sides ungreased.)

2 Sift flour and cocoa together 3 times.

3 In large heatproof bowl, whisk together eggs and ⅔ cup sugar. Place bowl over saucepan of barely simmering water (bowl should not touch water). Whisk constantly until eggs are lukewarm to the touch. Remove bowl from saucepan. Beat egg mixture at high speed 5 to 7 minutes or until mixture is cooled, tripled in bulk and resembles softly whipped cream.

4 Sift ⅓ of cocoa mixture over egg

mixture, folding gently until combined. Fold in remaining cocoa mixture in two parts. Add 1 cup of batter to warm butter; fold until thoroughly blended.

5 In medium bowl, combine clarified butter and 1 teaspoon vanilla. Add to remaining batter; fold just until incorporated. Pour batter into pan.

6 Bake 25 to 30 minutes or until toothpick inserted in center comes out clean. Cool cake in pan on wire rack 5 minutes. Run small knife around edges of cake to loosen. Cool completely.

7 Invert cake onto plate; remove parchment paper. (Génoise can be made up to 2 days ahead. Cover and refrigerate. Or freeze tightly wrapped up to 3 months.)

8 In large bowl, beat crème fraîche, whipping cream, 2 tablespoons sugar and 1½ teaspoons vanilla at medium speed until soft peaks form.

9 Slice cake horizontally into 2 layers. Place first layer, cut side up, on platter, cardboard cake circle or tart pan bottom. Brush with ¼ cup of the liqueur. Spread with ½ cup crème fraîche mixture. Top with 2½ cups of the raspberries. Spread 1 cup crème fraîche mixture over berries. Brush cut side of second cake layer with remaining ¼ cup liqueur. Place, moist side down, on crème fraîche mixture.

10 Frost top and sides with remaining crème fraîche mixture. Top with remaining ½ cup berries.*** Store in refrigerator.

TIPS *To make clarified butter, in small saucepan, melt 4 tablespoons unsalted butter over medium heat. Skim off foam that rises to the surface. Remove the clear butter, leaving the milky residue on bottom.

**If you cannot find crème fraîche at your grocery store, you can make your own. It should be started 1 to 3 days in advance as the thickening time varies. Heat 3 cups heavy or regular whipping cream (not ultrapasteurized) and 3 tablespoons buttermilk in medium saucepan over medium-low heat until mixture reaches 105°F. Let stand in a warm place, loosely covered, until thickened and slightly nutty. (This may take as little as 6 hours or as long as 36 hours.) Stir and taste every 6 to 8 hours. Do not let it mature too long or it will take on an unpleasant astringent flavor. Chill several hours before using. Extra crème fraîche may be made and refrigerated up to 10 days ahead.

***To sugar raspberries, just before serving gently rinse with water. Roll in sugar.

12 servings.

PER SERVING: 365 calories, 26.5 g total fat (15.5 g saturated fat), 4.5 g protein, 26.5 g carbohydrate, 155 mg cholesterol, 45 mg sodium, 3 g fiber.

Cocoa Basics

Two types There are two types of cocoa powder: natural (nonalkalized) and Dutch process (alkalized). Dutch-process cocoa has been treated with a chemical, such as potassium carbonate, to reduce the natural acidity of the cocoa beans. The process, called Dutching, softens the sharpness and fruitiness of the cocoa flavor and develops flavors that are toasty, espresso-like or sometimes even tea-like. Dutching also darkens the cocoa to an appetizing rich, deep reddish-brown color; extreme Dutching results in the distinctively flavored charcoal-black cocoa used to make Oreo cookies. Dutch-process cocoa may or may not be labeled as such, but "cocoa processed with alkali" should appear on the ingredient statement. Natural cocoa is typically labeled "cocoa."

Fat content Generally, higher fat content improves the flavor and quality of cocoa. Natural cocoas contain 10 to 12 percent fat, although superior-quality, high-fat natural cocoa is available with 22 to 24 percent fat. Dutch-process cocoa usually contains 15 to 24 percent fat. There is no need to alter recipes to accommodate different amounts of fat in cocoas.

Flavor differences Some cooks appreciate the unique mellow flavor of Dutch-process cocoa, while others prefer the sharper, fruitier flavor of natural cocoa. In most recipes, the two types are interchangeable. However, if a recipe contains leavenings (baking soda or baking powder), stick to the cocoa type that is specified. If there is no specific recommendation and the leavening is baking soda, use natural cocoa. In cake recipes containing leavenings, the wrong cocoa may result in a dense center streak of batter that does not rise; it can also produce a dark charcoal color with a pudding-like texture and soapy flavor.

Warm Chocolate Truffle Tart

This tart may be modest in appearance, with a filling that's just ½ inch thick, but its taste is truly rich, chocolaty and just plain decadent. The pastry, made with melted butter, bakes up crisp, sweet and buttery. The combination is unbeatable.

CRUST
- ½ cup unsalted butter
- ¼ cup sugar
- ¾ teaspoon vanilla
- ⅛ teaspoon salt
- 1 cup all-purpose flour

FILLING
- 5 tablespoons unsalted butter, cut up
- ½ cup sugar
- ¼ cup unsweetened cocoa
- 1 cup whipping cream
- 1¼ teaspoons instant espresso coffee powder
- ½ teaspoon vanilla
- 1 egg, lightly beaten

1 Heat oven to 350°F. Melt ½ cup butter in medium saucepan over medium heat. Remove from heat; stir in ¼ cup sugar, ¾ teaspoon vanilla and ⅛ teaspoon salt. Add flour; mix just until well combined.

2 Press dough in bottom and up sides of 9½-inch tart pan. Place pan on baking sheet. Bake 20 to 25 minutes or until deep golden brown.

3 Meanwhile, melt 5 tablespoons butter in same medium saucepan over medium heat. Add ½ cup sugar, cocoa and cream. Cook over medium heat, stirring until mixture is smooth and small bubbles begin to form around edges. Remove from heat; stir in coffee powder and ½ teaspoon vanilla.

4 Just before crust is done baking, whisk egg thoroughly into hot chocolate mixture. Remove crust from oven; pour filling into hot crust. Return to oven; bake an additional 10 to 12 minutes or until barely set. (Filling will quiver slightly when tapped at side.) Cool in pan on wire rack 25 minutes. Serve tart warm or at room temperature. Store in refrigerator.

8 servings.

PER SERVING: 400 calories, 29 g total fat (18 g saturated fat), 4 g protein, 33.5 g carbohydrate, 110 mg cholesterol, 55 mg sodium, 1.5 g fiber.

Warm Chocolate Truffle Tart

Doughnuts

Almond-Raspberry Doughnuts

A touch of decadence transforms a breakfast standard into a surprise ending.

Text and Recipes by Lisa Saltzman

We Americans have had a long-standing love affair with doughnuts. From the time they emerged as a breakfast treat, they've been embraced as quintessential comfort food. Whether glazed or chocolate, rolled in sprinkles or nuts, doughnuts are enjoyed by thousands of people every day.

Recently, the doughnut has developed a new persona. In restaurants throughout the country, it's being served for dessert, as an elegant ending to a meal. Doughnuts as dessert, you wonder? Just imagine small cakes—delicately flavored, moist and lightly fried—served with a rich sauce, ice cream, fruit compote or whipped cream. Once you've tried them, you'll appreciate them as much at the end of the day as you do at the beginning.

Almond-Raspberry Doughnuts

A rich almond torte and old-fashioned jelly-filled doughnuts were the inspirations for this luscious dessert that simply needs the accompaniment of soft whipped cream to complete it.

DOUGHNUTS
2 cups all-purpose flour
1½ teaspoons baking powder
½ teaspoon salt
3 oz. almond paste
½ cup sugar
¼ cup unsalted butter, room temperature
1 egg
⅓ cup milk
½ teaspoon vanilla
1 egg white, beaten
¼ cup strained raspberry preserves*
Vegetable oil for frying

TOPPING
½ cup whipping cream
3 tablespoons sugar
¼ teaspoon vanilla
½ cup strained raspberry preserves
1½ teaspoons kirsch, framboise, brandy or orange juice
1 tablespoon water

1 In medium bowl, stir together flour, baking powder and salt.

2 In large bowl, combine almond paste and ½ cup sugar; mix at low speed to break up almond paste into tiny pieces. Add butter; beat at medium speed 3 minutes or until fluffy. Add egg; beat until blended. At low speed, add milk and vanilla; beat until blended.

3 Stir in flour mixture. (Dough will be very soft and sticky.) Cover; let stand 20 minutes.

4 Line baking sheet with parchment paper. Place dough on well-floured surface; sprinkle dough with flour. With floured hands, pat dough to form ¼-inch-thick round. With greased and floured 1½-inch round cookie cutter, cut out circles; place on baking sheet. Brush half the circles with egg white.

5 Place ¼ cup preserves in small resealable plastic bag; seal bag. Make tiny cut in corner of bag with scissors. Squeeze ¼ teaspoon jam in center of each egg white-glazed circle. Place remaining circles over raspberry-topped ones. Press around edges to seal. If necessary, roll with hands to form balls; flatten to ½-inch thickness.

6 Heat 2 to 3 inches vegetable oil in heavy medium saucepan over medium heat to 375°F, using candy thermometer for accuracy. Deep-fry doughnuts 2 minutes or until golden brown, turning once. Remove doughnuts from oil; place on paper towels. (Doughnuts can be made up to 8 hours ahead. When ready to serve, warm doughnuts in 350°F oven for 5 minutes.)

Bittersweet Chocolate Doughnuts with Espresso Custard Sauce

7 In small bowl, beat cream at medium speed until soft peaks form. Add 3 tablespoons sugar and ¼ teaspoon vanilla; beat until slightly thicker. (Cream should still be soft and fall in soft mounds.)

8 In small saucepan, combine ½ cup preserves, kirsch and water. Heat until melted and smooth, stirring occasionally.

9 To serve, place 3 doughnuts on each dessert plate. Spoon whipped cream on plate beside doughnuts. Drizzle raspberry mixture over doughnuts and cream. Serve immediately. Refrigerate any leftover whipped cream.

TIP *Strain raspberry preserves through fine strainer to remove seeds. You may use seedless raspberry preserves, but the color and flavor are better in the regular preserves.

24 doughnuts; 8 servings.

PER SERVING: 460 calories, 19 g total fat (8 g saturated fat), 6.5 g protein, 68 g carbohydrate, 60 mg cholesterol, 275 mg sodium, 1.5 g fiber.

Bittersweet Chocolate Doughnuts with Espresso Custard Sauce

Chocolate and espresso are a winning combination in this dessert. Don't just limit it to dessert, though— a few chocolate doughnuts with a strong cup of coffee make a perfect mid-afternoon snack!

 2   cups all-purpose flour
 ½   cup Dutch-process cocoa
 1½ teaspoons baking powder
 ½   teaspoon salt
 2   eggs
 1½ cups sugar
 ¼   cup water
 ¼   cup unsalted butter, melted, cooled
 ½   teaspoon vanilla
     Vegetable oil for frying

TOPPING
 2   oz. bittersweet chocolate, chopped
     Espresso Custard Sauce

1 In medium bowl, stir together flour, cocoa, baking powder and salt.

2 In large heatproof bowl, whisk together eggs and 1 cup of the sugar. Place over saucepan of simmering water; stir until warm to the touch and sugar is dissolved. (Test by rubbing small amount between fingers—it should not be grainy.)

3 Remove from heat; beat at medium-high speed 3 minutes or until mixture is light, fluffy and pale yellow. Reduce speed to low; mix in water, butter and vanilla.

4 Stir in flour mixture. (Dough will be very soft and sticky.) Cover; let stand 20 minutes.

5 Line baking sheet with parchment paper. Place dough on well-floured surface; sprinkle dough with flour. With floured hands, pat dough to form ½-inch-thick round. With greased and floured 1½-inch round cookie cutter, cut out circles; place on baking sheet.

6 Heat 2 to 3 inches vegetable oil in heavy medium saucepan over medium heat to 375°F, using candy thermometer for accuracy. Deep fry doughnuts 2 minutes or until golden brown, turning once. Remove doughnuts from oil; place on paper towels. (Doughnuts can be made up to 8 hours ahead. When ready to serve, warm doughnuts in 350°F oven for 5 minutes.)

7 Place chocolate in small, heavy resealable plastic bag; seal bag. Place plastic bag in pan of barely simmering water to melt chocolate. When ready to use, make tiny cut in corner of bag with scissors.

8 To serve, pour 3 tablespoons Espresso Custard Sauce onto each dessert plate. Roll warm doughnuts in remaining ½ cup sugar. Place 3 doughnuts on sauce. Drizzle melted chocolate over sauce and doughnuts. Serve immediately.

36 doughnuts; 12 servings.

PER SERVING: 385 calories, 15.5 g total fat (6 g saturated fat), 7 g protein, 58 g carbohydrate, 160 mg cholesterol, 195 mg sodium, 2 g fiber.

Espresso Custard Sauce

 2¼ cups whole milk
 ⅓   cup espresso coffee beans
 6   egg yolks
 9   tablespoons sugar
 1½ teaspoons vanilla

1 In heavy medium saucepan, heat milk and espresso beans over medium heat until small bubbles form around edge. Remove from heat; cover and steep 30 to 40 minutes or until coffee flavor is strong.

2 Reheat over medium heat. In medium bowl, whisk egg yolks and sugar. Slowly whisk ½ cup warm milk mixture into yolks. Return yolk mixture to saucepan; cook over low heat until mixture coats spoon, stirring constantly. (Test by drawing finger across back of spoon; it should leave a clear trail in the custard. You can also test the custard with a candy thermometer; it will be properly cooked at 170°F to 175°F. Do not allow custard to boil; it will curdle.)

3 Immediately strain custard sauce through fine strainer into bowl. Place plastic wrap directly on custard surface to prevent skin from forming. Refrigerate until chilled. Stir in vanilla. Refrigerate any leftover sauce.

Ginger Doughnuts with Tropical Caramelized Bananas

Dipping these doughnuts in a tangy citrus-sugar glaze gives them additional moisture and a slightly crunchy exterior.

DOUGHNUTS
 1¾ cups all-purpose flour
 1½ teaspoons baking powder
 ½   teaspoon salt
 2   eggs
 ½   cup sugar
 ¼   cup unsalted butter, melted, cooled
 3   tablespoons milk
 1½ teaspoons grated fresh ginger
 1   teaspoon vanilla
     Vegetable oil for frying

Making Doughnuts

Traditional doughnuts take a variety of forms, but cake doughnuts are the best choice for dessert. They're leavened by baking powder and have denser textures than their yeast counterparts. Once the dough is made and shaped, the doughnuts are deep-fried, producing a light golden crust and a soft, moist interior.

Dough

The dough for these doughnuts is very soft and sticky, almost batter-like. In fact, you may be tempted to add more flour. Resist the temptation. Instead, let the dough stand for 20 minutes. It will become easier to work with, although it still may seem stickier than most dough.

Frying

The key to deep-frying is maintaining the temperature of the oil. If fried properly, the doughnut is lightly crusted on the outside and moist and cakey on the inside. If the temperature is too low, the doughnut absorbs the oil, making it heavy and greasy. If the temperature is too high, the doughnut fries too quickly on the outside and is raw on the inside.

To maintain the proper temperature of the oil:

- Start by heating the oil over medium heat. Avoid the temptation to heat it too quickly; if it gets too hot, it can be difficult to bring down the temperature.

- Use a candy thermometer. It allows you to control and maintain the temperature at 370°F to 375°F throughout the process. Watch the temperature carefully once the doughnuts are added to the oil; the heat may need to be adjusted occasionally to keep the oil close to 375°F.

- Fry only four or five doughnuts at a time so that you can maintain the temperature. Rushing the process by adding too many at once crowds the doughnuts and drops the temperature of the oil.

Equipment

With the exception of a good candy thermometer, you don't need special equipment for deep-frying. If you don't have a deep fryer, use a heavy saucepan that's at least 3 inches deep. At least 2 inches of oil are needed for doughnuts to fry evenly. A 2-quart saucepan works well for frying smaller doughnuts, and it saves on oil. In addition, a slotted spoon or screened spoon is preferred for turning and transferring the doughnuts to a cooling rack lined with paper towels.

Oil

Always use fresh oil when frying doughnuts. Reusing oil not only affects flavor but also the cooking process, temperature and frying time. Vegetable oil works best—it does not impart any flavor to the doughnuts and is relatively light.

GLAZE
- 1 cup sugar
- ¼ cup fresh lemon juice
- ¼ cup fresh orange juice

TOPPING
- Tropical Caramelized Bananas

1 In medium bowl, stir together flour, baking powder and salt.

2 In large heatproof bowl, whisk together eggs and ½ cup sugar. Place over saucepan of simmering water; stir until warm to the touch and sugar is dissolved. (Test by rubbing small amount between fingers—it should not be grainy.)

3 Remove from heat; beat at medium-high speed 3 minutes or until mixture is light, fluffy and pale yellow. Reduce speed to low; mix in butter, milk, ginger and vanilla.

4 Stir in flour mixture. (Dough will be very soft and sticky.) Cover; let stand 20 minutes. Meanwhile, in small saucepan, stir together all glaze ingredients. Cook over medium heat 3 to 4 minutes or until sugar dissolves; cool.

5 Line baking sheet with parchment paper. Place dough on well-floured surface; sprinkle dough with flour. With floured hands, pat dough to form ½-inch-thick round. With greased and floured 1½-inch round cookie cutter, cut out circles; place on baking sheet.

6 Heat 2 to 3 inches vegetable oil in heavy medium saucepan over medium heat to 375°F, using candy thermometer for accuracy. Deep-fry doughnuts 2 minutes or until golden brown, turning once. Remove doughnuts from oil; place on paper towels. (Doughnuts can be made up to 8 hours ahead. When ready to serve, warm doughnuts in 350°F oven for 5 minutes.)

7 To serve, dip warm doughnuts in glaze. Place 3 doughnuts on each dessert plate. Spoon warm Tropical Caramelized Bananas next to doughnuts. Serve immediately.

24 doughnuts; 8 servings.

PER SERVING: 765 calories, 29.5 g total fat (15 g saturated fat), 7.5 g protein, 115 g carbohydrate, 130 mg cholesterol, 350 mg sodium, 3 g fiber.

Cinnamon Doughnuts with Maple Syrup and Vanilla Ice Cream

Cinnamon doughnuts, topped with vanilla ice cream, maple syrup and walnuts, make a delicious dessert that highlights several of our country's most-favored foods.

DOUGHNUTS
1¾ cups all-purpose flour
1½ teaspoons baking powder
3 teaspoons cinnamon
½ teaspoon salt
½ teaspoon nutmeg
2 eggs
1 cup sugar
¼ cup unsalted butter, melted, cooled
3 tablespoons milk
½ teaspoon vanilla
Vegetable oil for frying

TOPPING
1 qt. vanilla ice cream
Maple Syrup Sauce (recipe follows)
½ cup finely chopped walnuts

1 In medium bowl, stir together flour, baking powder, 1 teaspoon of the cinnamon, salt and nutmeg.

2 In large heatproof bowl, whisk together eggs and ½ cup of the sugar. Place over saucepan of simmering water; stir until warm to the touch and sugar is dissolved. (Test by rubbing small amount between fingers—it should not be grainy.)

3 Remove from heat; beat at medium-high speed 3 minutes or until mixture is light, fluffy and pale yellow. Reduce speed to low; mix in butter, milk and vanilla.

4 Stir in flour mixture. (Dough will be very soft and sticky.) Cover; let stand 20 minutes. Meanwhile, stir together remaining ½ cup sugar and 2 teaspoons cinnamon in small bowl.

5 Line baking sheet with parchment paper. Place dough on well-floured surface; sprinkle dough with flour.

With floured hands, pat dough to form ½-inch-thick round. With greased and floured 1½-inch star-shaped cookie cutter, cut out stars; place on baking sheet.

6 Heat 2 to 3 inches vegetable oil in heavy medium saucepan over medium heat to 375°F, using candy thermometer for accuracy. Deep-fry doughnuts 2 minutes or until golden brown, turning once. Remove doughnuts from oil; place on paper towels. (Doughnuts can be made up to 8 hours ahead. When ready to serve, warm doughnuts in 350°F oven for 5 minutes.)

7 To serve, roll warm doughnuts in cinnamon sugar. Place 3 doughnuts on each dessert plate. Add scoop of ice cream to each. Pour 1 to 2 tablespoons Maple Syrup Sauce over doughnuts and ice cream. Sprinkle each with 1 tablespoon of the walnuts. Serve immediately.

24 doughnuts; 8 servings.

PER SERVING: 645 calories, 29.5 g total fat (13.5 g saturated fat), 8 g protein, 90 g carbohydrate, 115 mg cholesterol, 315 mg sodium, 1.5 g fiber.

Maple Syrup Sauce

½ cup sugar
2 tablespoons water
½ cup maple syrup
¼ cup unsalted butter, cut up

1 In small heavy saucepan, stir together sugar and water. Bring to a boil over medium-high heat. Continue boiling 6 to 8 minutes or until mixture is a rich caramel color.
2 Remove saucepan from heat. Slowly add maple syrup, whisking continuously. (Pour cautiously as syrup may spatter as it hits caramel.) If necessary, return to low heat to dissolve any hardened caramel.
3 Add butter in small pieces; whisk until melted.

Tropical Caramelized Bananas

SAUCE
3 tablespoons unsalted butter
¼ cup sugar
¼ cup fresh orange juice*
3 tablespoons dark rum or additional orange juice

BANANAS
¼ cup unsalted butter, cut up
¼ cup packed brown sugar
4 medium bananas, cut into ¼-inch slices
1½ teaspoons finely grated orange peel
½ teaspoon ground ginger

1 In medium saucepan, combine 3 tablespoons butter and sugar; cook over medium-high heat 4 to 6 minutes or until mixture is a rich golden brown, stirring constantly.

2 Reduce heat to low. Immediately add orange juice, whisking until any hardened caramel has dissolved. Add rum.

3 In medium skillet, melt ¼ cup butter and brown sugar over medium heat. Add sliced bananas; cook 1 minute or until thoroughly heated and completely coated with caramel, stirring gently. Stir in orange peel and ginger.

4 Pour orange sauce over caramelized bananas; stir gently to mix.

TIP *If squeezing oranges for juice, strain juice before measuring it. This makes a smoother caramel.

Tulip
Cups

Orange Tulip Cups with
Honeyed Blueberries and Oranges

Treat your dinner guests to an elegant ending—delicate cookie cups with dreamy fillings.

Text and Recipes by Susan G. Purdy

When creamy meets crunchy, wonderful things can happen. Who can resist, for example, the classic dessert of crème brûlée? It's that same union of contrasting textures that makes these desserts so inviting. Tulip-shaped cookies, paper-thin and crisp, cradle light, mousse-like fillings. Flavored gently with ginger, almonds, chocolate or fruit, they taste every bit as delicate as they look.

Desserts this special don't come without some attention to detail, but to make it easier for you, both the cookies and the fillings can be made in advance. At serving time, simply fill and garnish the cups. They make an elegant presentation and a perfect ending for a springtime dinner party.

Orange Tulip Cups with Honeyed Blueberries and Oranges

Bright flavors and contrasting colors give this dessert special appeal. Orange juice concentrate adds a sparkling tang to the cream cheese filling, and honey sweetens the berries for a delightful taste counterpoint. As an attractive garnish, you can cut long, thin strips of orange peel and wind them around a straw to give them a curl before serving.

ORANGE COOKIES
- ⅓ cup all-purpose flour
- ⅓ cup sugar
- ⅛ teaspoon salt
- 2 tablespoons unsalted butter, melted, cooled
- 2 tablespoons vegetable oil
- 1 teaspoon grated orange peel
- 1 teaspoon vanilla
- 1 teaspoon pure orange extract
- 2 egg whites

ORANGE CREAM
- 12 oz. cream cheese, softened
- ¼ cup sugar
- 2 tablespoons frozen orange juice concentrate, thawed
- 2 tablespoons orange-flavored liqueur or orange juice
- 1 tablespoon grated orange peel

BERRIES
- 4 cups fresh blueberries
- 1 orange, peeled, cut into segments
- 2 tablespoons warm honey
- 1 teaspoon grated orange peel
  Dash nutmeg

1 Heat oven to 350°F. Spray 2 baking sheets with nonstick cooking spray.

2 In medium bowl, stir together flour, sugar and salt. In another medium bowl, whisk together all remaining cookie ingredients. Add to flour mixture, whisking until smooth.

3 For each cookie, spoon 1½ tablespoons batter onto baking sheet; spread evenly to 6-inch round, eliminating any holes. Make only 2 cookies per baking sheet, placing at least 1 inch apart.

4 Bake one sheet at a time 6 to 8 minutes or just until tops are dry and light brown, with golden-brown edges. Place cookies in 6-oz. custard cups. Place second custard cup over cookies to form cups. Remove from molds; set on cooling rack. Cool completely. Repeat using remaining batter.

5 In food processor, combine all orange cream ingredients; process until smooth. Refrigerate up to 8 hours. Mixture should be soft enough to spoon easily, like a thick pudding. If too stiff, beat in a few tablespoons of orange juice just before serving.

6 In medium bowl, lightly toss together all berry ingredients. Cover; refrigerate until ready to serve.

7 To serve, place tulip cups on individual dessert plates. Fill each with

Almond Tulip Cups with Chocolate Mousse

about 3 tablespoons orange cream. Top with berry mixture.

8 servings.

PER SERVING: 370 calories, 21.5 g total fat (11.5 g saturated fat), 5.5 g protein, 39.5 g carbohydrate, 55 mg cholesterol, 180 mg sodium, 2.5 g fiber.

Ginger Tulip Cups with Peaches and Ginger Cream

This ginger-peach combination is livened by the sharp, clean taste of fresh, powdered and candied, or crystallized, ginger. To peel peaches easily, place the whole fruit in boiling water for about 2 minutes, then remove it with a slotted spoon to a bowl of cold water. Skins will slip off easily. Nectarines can be substituted for the peaches, but don't peel the nectarines. If slicing the fruit in advance, toss it with 2 or 3 tablespoons of orange juice to avoid discoloring. Drain the slices on paper towels before serving.

GINGER COOKIES
- ⅓ cup all-purpose flour
- ⅓ cup sugar
- 1½ teaspoons ground ginger
- ⅛ teaspoon salt
- 2 tablespoons unsalted butter, melted, cooled
- 2 tablespoons vegetable oil
- 2 teaspoons grated fresh ginger
- 1 teaspoon vanilla
- 2 egg whites

GINGER CREAM
- 1½ cups heavy whipping cream
- 3 tablespoons powdered sugar
- ½ teaspoon ground ginger
- 2 tablespoons minced crystallized ginger

FRUIT
- 4 cups sliced peeled peaches or nectarines

1 Heat oven to 350°F. Spray 2 baking sheets with nonstick cooking spray.

2 In large bowl, stir together flour, ⅓ cup sugar, 1½ teaspoons ground ginger and salt. In medium bowl, whisk together all remaining cookie ingredients. Add to dry ingredients, whisking until smooth.

3 For each cookie, spoon 1½ tablespoons batter onto baking sheet; spread evenly to 6-inch round, eliminating any holes. Make only 2 cookies per baking sheet, placing at least 1 inch apart.

4 Bake one sheet at a time 6 to 8 minutes or just until tops are dry and pale, with golden-brown edges. Place cookies in 6-oz. custard cups. Place second custard cup over cookies to form cup shape. Remove from molds; set on cooling rack. Cool completely. Repeat using remaining batter.

5 To make ginger cream, in large bowl, beat cream at medium-high speed until soft peaks form. Add 3 tablespoons powdered sugar and ½ teaspoon ground ginger; beat at medium-high speed until stiff peaks form. Fold in 2 tablespoons crystallized ginger. Refrigerate up to 2 hours.

6 To serve, place tulip cups on individual dessert plates. Fill each with scant ⅓ cup ginger cream. Top with peaches.

8 servings.

PER SERVING: 300 calories, 20 g total fat (12.5 g saturated fat), 3.5 g protein, 29.5 g carbohydrate, 65 mg cholesterol, 95 mg sodium, 2 g fiber.

Almond Tulip Cups with Chocolate Mousse

The dense, rich chocolate mousse pairs perfectly with delicate, almond-flavored cookie cups. For an attractive presentation, place the mousse in a large pastry bag with a star tip and pipe it into the cups.

ALMOND COOKIES
- ⅓ cup all-purpose flour
- ⅓ cup sugar
- ⅛ teaspoon salt
- 2 tablespoons unsalted butter, melted, cooled
- 2 tablespoons vegetable oil
- 1 teaspoon vanilla
- ½ teaspoon almond extract
- 2 egg whites
- 3 tablespoons sliced almonds

CHOCOLATE MOUSSE
- 6 oz. semisweet or bittersweet chocolate, finely chopped
- 1½ cups heavy whipping cream
- 2 tablespoons light corn syrup
- 3 egg yolks

GARNISH
- ¼ cup sliced almonds, toasted*

1 Heat oven to 350°F. Spray 2 baking sheets with nonstick cooking spray.

2 In medium bowl, stir together flour, sugar and salt. In another medium bowl, whisk together all remaining cookie ingredients except 3 tablespoons almonds. Add to flour mixture, whisking until smooth.

3 For each cookie, spoon 1½ tablespoons batter onto baking sheet; spread evenly to 6-inch round, eliminating any holes. Make only 2 cookies per baking sheet, placing at least 1 inch apart. Sprinkle each cookie with ⅛ of the sliced almonds.

4 Bake one sheet at a time 6 to 8 minutes or just until tops are dry and light brown, with golden-brown edges. Immediately place cookies in 6-oz. custard cups. Place second custard cup over cookies to form cup shape. Remove from molds; set on cooling rack. Cool completely. Repeat using remaining batter.

5 To make chocolate mousse, place chocolate in heatproof medium bowl. Bring 1 inch water to a boil in medium saucepan. Remove from heat. Place bowl of chocolate over saucepan (bowl should not touch water). Let stand until melted. Stir. Remove from heat; set aside to cool.

6 In small heavy saucepan over medium-low heat, whisk together ½ cup of the cream, corn syrup and egg yolks. Cook, whisking constantly, 5 to 6 minutes or until mixture is thick, covers back of spoon and reaches 160°F on instant-read thermometer. (Be careful not to overcook.)

7 Strain yolk mixture into chocolate. Immediately whisk briskly, making chocolate shiny and satin-smooth. Cool to 80°F to 85°F. (Mixture should feel comfortable to the touch.)

Making Tulip Cups

Baking and shaping the tulip cookie cups is not difficult, but it does require a technique that is best learned through practice. The cups are baked into flat, round cookies and then, while still warm, molded between two custard cups into a tulip shape.

Baking For each cookie, spoon 1½ tablespoons of the batter onto a greased baking sheet. To spread evenly into a 6-inch circle, first spread the batter into a 6-inch cross using an offset spatula or spoon. This gives you an outline from which to work. Then spread the batter into a 6-inch circle. So that you'll have time to mold the cookies while they're still warm, bake just two on a baking sheet, and bake one sheet at a time. Regrease the pan between batches.

Bake one cookie first, to test for correct baking time. If the cookies are white or pale and underbaked, the cups will not get crisp when cooled. If they are overbaked, they may break when you try to lift them from the pan or shape them. Ideally, they should bake until the outer edges are golden brown. After cooling, properly baked cups should be crisp to the touch.

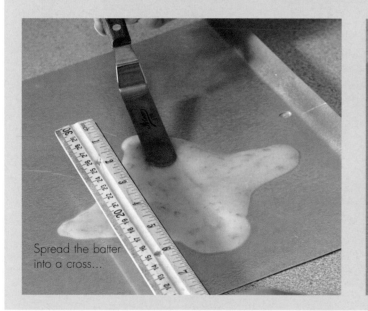

Spread the batter into a cross...

...then into a circle.

8 In large bowl, beat remaining 1 cup cream at medium-high speed until soft peaks form. Fold cooled chocolate mixture into whipped cream. Cover; refrigerate up to 8 hours. Bring to room temperature before serving.

9 To serve, place tulip cups on individual dessert plates. Fill each with chocolate mousse; sprinkle with toasted almonds.

TIP *To toast almonds, place on baking sheet; bake at 375°F for 6 minutes or until deep golden brown.

8 servings.

PER SERVING: 410 calories, 31.5 g total fat (17 g saturated fat), 6 g protein, 29.5 g carbohydrate, 145 mg cholesterol, 85 mg sodium, 2 g fiber.

Chocolate Tulip Cups with Vanilla Cream and Fresh Berries

Before you're ready to make the cream filling, note that the yogurt must first be drained in a strainer placed over a bowl for about 30 minutes. If you're using strawberries, they can be cut and sugared in advance; raspberries should be prepared at the last minute.

CHOCOLATE COOKIES
- ½ cup sugar
- ⅓ cup all-purpose flour
- 2 tablespoons Dutch-process cocoa*
- ⅛ teaspoon salt
  Dash cinnamon
- 2 tablespoons butter, melted
- 2 tablespoons vegetable oil
- 1 teaspoon vanilla
- 2 egg whites

VANILLA CREAM
- 1 cup vanilla yogurt
- 1 (8-oz.) pkg. cream cheese, softened
- 2 tablespoons sugar
- 1 teaspoon vanilla

BERRIES
- 3 cups fresh raspberries or sliced strawberries
- 1 to 2 tablespoons sugar, if desired
  Powdered sugar

1 Heat oven to 350°F. Spray 2 baking sheets with nonstick cooking spray.

2 In large bowl, stir together ½ cup

Shaping As soon as you remove the baking sheet from the oven, use a spatula to ease one cookie at a time off the sheet. Place the cookie over a custard cup and put another custard cup on top of the cookie. Don't force the cup; let gravity slowly pull it down. With the top custard cup in place, shape the ruffled edge of the tulip cup. This entire molding process should take only a few seconds. After a minute or two, when they are cool and crisp, place the tulip cups on a wire rack.

If the cookies cool or stick to the baking sheet before you have time to lift them off, return the pan to the oven for a minute or two to warm them until they are flexible.

Making ahead In cool, dry weather, you can bake the cups three to four days ahead and store them in an airtight container.

In humid weather, the cups may lose their shape and start to flatten. If this happens, position each limp cookie in the cup of a muffin pan, easing it down into the cup shape. Warm them in a 350°F oven for 3 to 5 minutes. Allow the cups to cool completely before removing them from the pan. Fill and serve immediately.

Place the second cup over the warm cookie.

Use your hands to shape the edge.

sugar, flour, cocoa, salt and cinnamon. In small bowl, whisk together all remaining cookie ingredients. Add butter mixture to dry ingredients, whisking until smooth.

3 For each cookie, spoon 1½ tablespoons batter onto baking sheet; spread evenly to 6-inch round, eliminating any holes. Make only 2 cookies per baking sheet, placing at least 1 inch apart.

4 Bake one sheet at a time 8 to 10 minutes or until tops are dry, with slightly darker edges. Place cookies in 6-oz. custard cups. Place second custard cup over cookies to form cup shape. Remove from molds; set on cooling rack. Cool completely. Repeat using remaining batter.

5 To make vanilla cream, drain vanilla yogurt in strainer set over bowl 30 minutes; discard liquid. In medium bowl, beat cream cheese at medium speed until soft. Add strained yogurt, 2 tablespoons sugar and 1 teaspoon vanilla; beat until smooth. Refrigerate up to 8 hours. In medium bowl, toss berries with 1 to 2 tablespoons sugar.

6 To serve, place tulip cups on individual dessert plates. Fill each with about ¼ cup vanilla cream. Top with berries; lightly sprinkle with powdered sugar.

TIP *Unsweetened cocoa can be used if Dutch-process is unavailable.

8 servings.

PER SERVING: 305 calories, 16.5 g total fat (10 g saturated fat), 6 g protein, 35.5 g carbohydrate, 50 mg cholesterol, 160 mg sodium, 4 g fiber.

Cool and
Creamy

White Chocolate-Boysenberry Mousse

Take a refresher course in what's cool with these light and creamy desserts.

Text and Recipes by Lisa Saltzman

In summer, it's a whole new scene when it comes to food, especially desserts. The rich, heavier sweets that delighted us during winter are as out of place as a down coat on a 90-degree day. But giving up dessert is not an option—at least not at my house.

The hot outdoor temperatures demand something cold that doesn't heat up the kitchen. So I turn to my favorite warm-weather desserts—chilled or frozen soufflés and mousses. They have everything I like in a dessert this time of year: Gelatin and whipped cream keep them light, and little or no cooking keeps them uncomplicated. And lucky for me, they can be prepared well in advance. Of course, the best thing of all is their refreshing taste.

White Chocolate-Boysenberry Mousse

Avoid the temptation to overbeat the cream for the mousse. The cream will continue to be "whipped" as it is folded into the base and can become curdled-looking if too stiff.

MOUSSE
- 3 cups boysenberries, raspberries and/or blackberries
- ⅔ cup sugar
- 2 teaspoons unflavored gelatin
- 2 tablespoons cold water
- 9 oz. white chocolate, chopped
- 5 tablespoons milk
- 1 teaspoon vanilla
- 3 cups whipping cream

GARNISH
- 3 cups boysenberries, raspberries or blackberries

1 Puree 3 cups boysenberries in food processor until smooth. Press puree through fine strainer to remove seeds. Stir in sugar. (You should have about 1½ cups puree.)

2 In small saucepan, sprinkle gelatin over water; let stand 5 minutes to soften. Dissolve gelatin over very low heat, stirring occasionally. Pour into medium bowl. Stir in 1 cup boysenberry puree. Reserve remaining ½ cup puree for sauce.

3 In microwave-safe bowl, combine white chocolate and milk. Microwave on low 2 to 3 minutes or until melted. Stir until smooth. Cool to room temperature. Stir in vanilla.

4 In large bowl, beat whipping cream at medium-high speed until soft peaks form. Do not overbeat; cream should just hold soft shape

Frozen Apricot Mousse with Bing Cherry Compote

and still be loose in bowl. Fold half of whipped cream into boysenberry mixture; fold remaining half into white chocolate mixture.

5 Pour half of boysenberry mousse into 8-cup glass bowl. Pour half of white chocolate mousse over berry mousse. Repeat. With knife, swirl mixtures together to create pattern. Do not overstir. (You won't be able to see pattern until you scoop out dessert.) Cover; refrigerate 3 to 4 hours or until set.

6 To serve, scoop 1 to 2 large spoonfuls of mousse onto each plate. Garnish with boysenberries; drizzle with reserved sauce. Store in refrigerator.

10 servings.

PER SERVING: 535 calories, 38.5 g total fat (23.5 g saturated fat), 5 g protein, 45.5 g carbohydrate, 105 mg cholesterol, 65 mg sodium, 1.5 g fiber.

Frozen Apricot Mousse with Bing Cherry Compote

Apricots and cherries are one of nature's perfect marriages. Choose apricots that are soft, not mushy, and have a sweet aroma. If desired, this same mousse can be made with peaches, plums or nectarines.

MOUSSE
- 1 lb. apricots (about 7 medium), halved
- ½ teaspoon apricot brandy or rum, if desired
- 3 egg yolks
- ½ cup plus 2 tablespoons sugar
- ¼ cup water
- 1¼ cups whipping cream
- ½ teaspoon vanilla

COMPOTE
- 1½ lbs. fresh Bing cherries, pitted
- ⅔ cup sugar
- 2 tablespoons port or water

1 Lightly moisten bottom and sides of 9x5-inch loaf pan. (This will help keep plastic wrap in place.) Line with plastic wrap. Place apricot halves, flesh-side down, in medium saucepan. Cover; cook over medium to medium-low heat 5 to 10 minutes

or until softened and tender. (If apricots are dry, add a little water to saucepan to keep them from scorching.) Puree apricots in food processor until smooth. Measure 1½ cups puree; cool. Reserve any remaining puree for another use. Stir in apricot brandy.

2 In heatproof large bowl, whisk together egg yolks, ½ cup of the sugar and water. Place over saucepan of simmering water (bowl should not touch water). Cook 4 to 5 minutes or until light, slightly thickened and temperature reaches 160°F, whisking constantly. Remove from heat. Beat at medium speed until cooled to room temperature. Fold in apricot puree.

3 In medium bowl, beat whipping cream, remaining 2 tablespoons sugar and vanilla at medium-high speed until soft peaks form. Fold ¾ of the cream into apricot mixture.

4 Pour half (about 2 cups) of the apricot mousse into loaf pan. Freeze 20 minutes. (Refrigerate remaining apricot mousse and cream.) Carefully spread remaining cream over frozen mousse. Freeze an additional 20 minutes.

5 Pour remaining apricot mousse over cream. Cover with plastic wrap; freeze 5 to 6 hours or until firm.

6 Meanwhile, place cherries and ⅔ cup sugar in large saucepan. Cook over medium heat 4 to 5 minutes or until cherries begin to juice slightly. Stir in port; boil 1 minute. Refrigerate until cool. Serve at room temperature or chilled.

7 To serve, unmold mousse onto serving platter; remove plastic wrap. Slice and serve with compote. Store in freezer.

12 servings.

PER SERVING: 235 calories, 9.5 g total fat (5.5 g saturated fat), 2.5 g protein, 36.5 g carbohydrate, 80 mg cholesterol, 10 mg sodium, 2 g fiber.

Iced Lemon Soufflé

A cold soufflé is actually not a soufflé at all, but it gives the visual impression of a light dessert that has risen above the soufflé dish. It creates a dramatic presentation, and, though slightly time-consuming, it can be prepared well in advance. This dessert is ideal for a large group of people and can be made throughout the year. If available, try Meyer lemons in the winter months for brighter flavor.

- 2 tablespoons unflavored gelatin
- ¼ cup cold water
- 8 eggs, separated
- 2¼ cups sugar
- 2 tablespoons grated lemon peel
- 1 cup fresh lemon juice
- 1¾ cups whipping cream
- 2 pints fresh strawberries, sliced (4 cups)

1 Prepare 2-quart soufflé mold by wrapping double thickness of foil or parchment paper tightly around mold, extending foil 2 to 3 inches above mold. Staple in place; spray with nonstick cooking spray.

2 Sprinkle gelatin over water in small metal bowl to soften. In heatproof large bowl, whisk together egg yolks, 1 cup of the sugar, lemon peel and lemon juice. Place bowl over saucepan of simmering water (bowl should not touch water); whisk mixture constantly 6 to 8 minutes or until light colored, thickened and temperature reaches 160°F. Remove from heat; beat at medium speed until cooled to room temperature.

3 Place bowl of gelatin over saucepan of simmering water; melt gently until liquid. Stir into lemon mixture.

4 In large bowl, beat whipping cream at medium-high speed until soft peaks form. Fold into lemon mixture.

5 In another heatproof large bowl, whisk together egg whites and 1 cup of the sugar. Place bowl over saucepan of simmering water (bowl should not touch water); whisk constantly until sugar is dissolved and mixture is hot to the touch, 2 to 3 minutes. (To test, rub small amount of egg white mixture between fingers; it should feel silky and smooth.) Remove from heat. Beat at medium speed 4 to 5 minutes or until stiff peaks form. Fold into lemon-cream mixture.

6 Pour into soufflé dish. Mixture should be 1 to 2 inches above rim of dish. Refrigerate 3 to 4 hours or until set.

7 Before serving, toss strawberries with remaining ¼ cup sugar; let stand 10 to 15 minutes. Scoop 1 to 2 large spoonfuls of lemon soufflé onto each plate. Spoon strawberries over soufflé.

16 servings.

PER SERVING: 240 calories, 11 g total fat (6 g saturated fat), 4.5 g protein, 33 g carbohydrate, 135 mg cholesterol, 45 mg sodium, 1 g fiber.

Almond Panna Cotta

Panna cotta is an Italian dessert similar to a flan. Rather than using eggs to bind it together, however, it requires gelatin. Though the name panna cotta means "cooked cream," there is relatively little cooking involved, which makes it an ideal dessert to prepare on a hot summer day.

    1   cup whole unblanched almonds
    3   cups whipping cream
    ¾   cup plus 2 tablespoons
        sugar
    4½ teaspoons unflavored
        gelatin
    1½ cups whole milk
    ½   teaspoon almond extract
    4   nectarines

1 Heat oven to 375°F. Line bottom of 8 (6-oz.) ramekins with parchment paper. Place almonds on baking sheet. Bake 8 to 10 minutes or until lightly browned. Cool; chop coarsely.

2 In medium saucepan, combine cream, ¾ cup of the sugar and almonds. Bring to a boil over medium-high heat, stirring occasionally. Remove from heat. Cover; let stand 15 minutes.

3 Meanwhile, in medium bowl, sprinkle gelatin over milk; let stand at least 5 minutes to soften.

4 Reheat almond-cream mixture until hot. Add milk mixture; stir to dissolve gelatin. Add almond extract. Strain through fine strainer into large measuring cup or pitcher.

5 Pour mixture into 8 (6-oz.) ramekins. Refrigerate 2 hours or until set. (Panna cotta can be made up to 24 hours ahead. Cover and refrigerate.)

6 To serve, slice nectarines into ¼-inch slices; place in large bowl. Toss with remaining 2 tablespoons sugar. Let stand 10 to 15 minutes. To unmold custards, run knife around edges and dip bottoms of ramekins in hot water. Serve nectarines over panna cotta. Store in refrigerator.

8 servings.

PER SERVING: 415 calories, 29.5 g total fat (18.5 g saturated fat), 5 g protein, 34.5 g carbohydrate, 105 mg cholesterol, 55 mg sodium, 1 g fiber.

Frozen Espresso Caramel Parfait

Inspired by friends who love caramel café lattes, this frozen parfait has the creaminess of ice cream without needing to use an ice cream machine.

    2   cups whipping cream
    2½ teaspoons vanilla
    8   egg yolks
    ½   cup hot coffee
    2   teaspoons espresso coffee
        powder
    1   cup plus 2 tablespoons sugar
    ¼   cup water
    1   oz. semisweet chocolate

1 In large bowl, beat 1½ cups of the whipping cream and 2 teaspoons of the vanilla at medium-high speed until soft peaks form. Refrigerate.

2 In heatproof large bowl, beat egg yolks at medium-high speed 4 to 5 minutes or until thick, pale yellow and mixture holds a 1- to 2-second ribbon. (To test for ribbon, drop spoonful of mixture back onto surface; spoonful should hold its shape for at least 1 to 2 seconds before disappearing into mixture.) Continue beating at low speed while making caramel.

3 In small bowl, combine hot coffee and espresso coffee powder. In small saucepan, combine 1 cup of the sugar and water. Bring to a rolling boil over medium-high heat, swirling, if necessary, to blend. Boil 4 to 7

minutes until mixture begins to turn a light caramel color.

4 Remove from heat; this will slow down the caramelization process and give you more control. Allow mixture to continue caramelizing. When mixture reaches a rich caramel color, place saucepan in sink; carefully pour coffee-espresso mixture into caramel, stirring constantly.

5 Immediately return to heat; bring to a boil, dissolving any hardened caramel. When caramel is liquid again, pour into egg yolks in slow steady stream, beating at medium-high speed until combined. Place bowl over saucepan of simmering water (bowl should not touch water). Whisk 2 to 4 minutes or until temperature reaches 160°F. Remove from heat. Beat at medium-high speed 8 to 10 minutes or until mixture has cooled and thickened.

6 When caramel mixture is cool, immediately fold in whipped cream. Pour into 8 (6-oz.) parfait or stemmed glasses. Cover with plastic wrap; freeze at least 6 hours or overnight.

7 To serve, in medium bowl, beat remaining ½ cup whipping cream at medium-high speed until soft peaks form. Add remaining 2 tablespoons sugar and remaining ½ teaspoon vanilla, beating until stiff peaks form. With pastry bag fitted with star tip, pipe whipped cream onto each parfait. With vegetable peeler, shave chocolate over whipped cream. Store in refrigerator.

8 servings.

PER SERVING: 365 calories, 24.5 g total fat (14 g saturated fat), 4.5 g protein, 33 g carbohydrate, 280 mg cholesterol, 30 mg sodium, .5 g fiber.

Creamy Desserts Without Raw Eggs

Cold mousse and soufflé desserts traditionally rely on whipped raw egg whites to make them light yet firm. But because raw eggs could be contaminated with salmonella, several alternative methods have been used in these recipes to achieve the right texture without the health risks. Two methods cook the eggs to kill the bacteria. This involves both time and temperature. The other method uses gelatin and whipped cream instead of eggs to get the same effect.

Water bath method This technique is used in Frozen Apricot Mousse. Place the egg yolks, sugar and water in a mixing bowl set over a pan of simmering water. The bottom of the bowl should not touch the water. Whisk continuously for 4 to 5 minutes—the mixture will become thick and light-colored. After cooking, cool to room temperature by beating continuously with a mixer.

Italian meringue method For this technique, used in Frozen Espresso Caramel Parfait, a hot sugar syrup (in this case, caramel) is poured into egg yolks as they're being whipped. Timing is key with this method, and it helps to have a stand mixer or another person to help you. First beat the egg yolks with a mixer until they triple in volume. Pour the espresso caramel in a steady stream into the beaten eggs. Place the mixing bowl over a pan of simmering water and whisk until the temperature of the mixture reaches 160°F. Return the bowl to the mixer, and beat it until it has cooled and thickened.

Gelatin and whipping cream The remaining recipes use a combination of gelatin and whipped cream for a light, firm texture. To use gelatin, it must first be softened. Sprinkle the gelatin into a cool liquid and let it stand for at least five minutes. Then heat it over low heat or place it over a pan of simmering water to dissolve it gently. The bottom of the pan should be cool enough to touch with your bare hands. After the gelatin has dissolved and while it is still warm, it must be added to the mousse base. It sets as soon as it gets cold.

Whipping the cream properly is the key to making these desserts smooth and creamy. Whipped cream continues to thicken as it's folded into the base mixture, so it's important not to overwhip it initially. To beat the cream properly, whip it at medium speed until it just begins to hold a soft shape. It should still be slightly loose in the bowl but not liquid, and it should have the consistency of a soft pudding.

Clafouti

Country French Blackberry Clafouti

Fruit is the foundation of this simple, beloved French dessert.

Text and Recipes by Beth Hensperger

Country French Blackberry Clafouti

After baking, this clafouti ends up unevenly puffy and rustic-looking, rather like it has just emerged from a wood-fire oven. Serve the dessert warm from the oven in fat wedges, with lightly whipped cream.

There is nothing fancy or sophisticated about the country fruit dessert called clafouti (pronounced kla-foo-TEE), but you're bound to adore it nevertheless. In France, it's a much-loved dessert, and some variation of it is part of every French cook's repertoire.

Clafouti is made with fresh fruit that's topped with a pancake-like batter and baked in a shallow-sided baking dish. It originally hails from the Limousin region of central France, where it is made with stemmed, unpitted, fresh sweet cherries in the spring (the pits add an almond-like essence to the flavor). But this is a dessert that's made for improvisation. The batter adapts well to a wide number of fresh summer fruits, such as peaches, apples, figs and berries.

Use these recipes to get started. Then experiment with your own variations. You'll soon discover why it's a favorite in France.

CLAFOUTI
- 2 tablespoons unsalted butter
- ¾ cup all-purpose flour
- ½ cup sugar
- ⅛ teaspoon salt
- ¾ cup whole milk
- ¼ cup whipping cream
- 2 tablespoons amaretto liqueur or ¾ teaspoon almond extract
- 2 teaspoons vanilla
- 4 eggs
- 2 cups fresh blackberries

WHIPPED CREAM
- 1 cup whipping cream
- 1 tablespoon sugar

1 Heat oven to 425°F. Place butter in 10-inch round or oval baking dish. Place baking dish in oven 2 to 4 minutes or just until butter is melted.

2 In large bowl, stir together flour, ½ cup sugar and salt. Slowly whisk in milk and ¼ cup whipping cream, blending until smooth. Add liqueur and vanilla. Whisk in eggs one at a time until well-blended. Batter will be thin.

3 Remove baking dish from oven. Tilt pan to coat bottom and sides with melted butter. Place blackberries in single layer in baking dish. Immediately pour batter over berries.

Individual Buttermilk Clafoutis with Plums

4 Return baking dish to oven; bake 12 minutes. Reduce oven temperature to 350°F. Bake an additional 35 to 45 minutes or until puffed, very dark brown around edges and knife inserted in center comes out clean. Cool 10 to 20 minutes before serving.

5 Meanwhile, in small bowl, combine 1 cup whipping cream and 1 tablespoon sugar; beat at medium-high speed until soft peaks form. Serve over warm clafouti. Refrigerate leftovers.

6 servings.

PER SERVING: 420 calories, 24 g total fat (13.5 g saturated fat), 8.5 g protein, 42 g carbohydrate, 210 mg cholesterol, 120 mg sodium, 3 g fiber.

Individual Buttermilk Clafoutis with Plums

The combination of plums and Grand Marnier is especially delightful in these single-portion clafoutis. If you'd like to purchase special dishes to make these, look for shallow 4½-inch round, fluted, ovenproof porcelain tart dishes or 5-inch individual gratin dishes, made by Apilco and Emile Henry.

 1 lb. firm but ripe purple plums (about 4), cut into ½-inch slices
 ½ cup sugar
 3 tablespoons Grand Marnier liqueur or orange juice
 ¼ cup unsalted butter, cut into 8 pieces
 1 cup all-purpose flour
 ½ teaspoon baking powder
 ⅛ teaspoon salt
 ¾ cup buttermilk
 ¾ cup half-and-half
 1 teaspoon grated orange peel
 ½ teaspoon vanilla
 3 eggs
    Powdered sugar

WHIPPED CREAM
 1 cup whipping cream
 ⅓ cup crème fraîche or sour cream
 2 tablespoons cassis syrup*
 2 tablespoons sugar

1 Place plums in medium bowl. Sprinkle with ¼ cup of the sugar and the liqueur. Partially cover; let stand at room temperature 1 hour or up to 2 hours.

2 Heat oven to 400°F. Place 1 piece butter in each of 8 (4½-inch) round shallow fluted ceramic tart pans. Place on baking sheet. Place in oven to melt butter while preparing batter.

3 In large bowl, stir together flour, remaining ¼ cup sugar, baking powder and salt. Slowly whisk in buttermilk, half-and-half, orange peel and vanilla, blending until smooth. Whisk in eggs one at a time until well-blended.

4 Drain plums, adding liquid to batter; beat at medium speed 1 minute or until frothy. Batter will be thin.

5 Remove baking sheet with pans from oven. With pastry brush, coat bottom and sides of pans with melted butter. Place plum slices in single layer in pans. Pour about ½ cup batter over fruit in each pan.

6 Return baking sheet with pans to oven; bake 8 minutes. Reduce oven temperature to 350°F. Bake an additional 20 to 25 minutes or until puffed, golden brown and knife inserted in center comes out clean. Remove from oven; immediately sprinkle each dessert with powdered sugar. Cool 10 minutes before serving.

7 Meanwhile, in medium bowl, beat together all whipped cream ingredients at medium-high speed until soft peaks form. Cover; refrigerate until serving time. Serve with warm clafoutis. Refrigerate leftovers.

TIPS *Cassis syrup is made from black currants and can be found in specialty stores. Other fruit syrups, often used for flavoring coffee, can be used.

This can also be made in a 12-inch ceramic mold. Melt only 2 tablespoons butter in mold. (Omit heating and using baking sheet.) Fill with custard; bake at 400°F for 15 minutes. Reduce oven temperature to 350°F. Bake an additional 45 minutes or until puffed, dark golden brown and knife inserted in center comes out clean. Follow remainder of recipe as written.

8 servings.

PER SERVING: 400 calories, 22.5 g total fat (13 g saturated fat), 7 g protein, 42.5 g carbohydrate, 145 mg cholesterol, 135 mg sodium, 1 g fiber.

Apple and Dried Plum Clafouti Tart

This clafouti is a bit different from the traditional one in that it's baked in a flaky pastry shell, easily made with frozen puff pastry. The filling features apples and prunes, a combination that is beloved in French baking.

 1 (17.3-oz.) pkg. frozen puff pastry, thawed
 25 pitted dried plums (prunes) from 1 (12-oz.) pkg.
 ¾ cup water
 2 tablespoons brandy or apple juice
 1½ tablespoons butter
 2 large baking apples (such as Fuji, Golden Delicious or Granny Smith), peeled, cut into ¼-inch slices
 3 tablespoons packed light brown sugar
 ¼ teaspoon cinnamon
 1 cup crème fraîche or sour cream
 2 eggs
 3 tablespoons all-purpose flour
 ⅛ teaspoon salt

1 Place 1 sheet puff pastry on lightly floured surface. Top with second sheet of pastry. Roll to 13-inch square. Place in 10-inch tart pan; press pastry, without stretching, into bottom and up sides of pan. Press rolling pin over top to trim excess. Cover; refrigerate while preparing filling.

2 In small microwave-safe bowl, combine dried plums, water and brandy. Microwave on high 3 minutes. Partially cover; let stand at room temperature 30 minutes. Drain, reserving 2 tablespoons liquid.

3 Melt butter in medium skillet over medium heat. Add apples; cook

5 minutes or until softened, stirring to coat apples with butter. Sprinkle with 1 tablespoon of the brown sugar and cinnamon; cook and stir until combined. Remove from heat; refrigerate until cool.

4 Meanwhile, heat oven to 400°F. Place baking sheet on middle oven rack to heat. In small bowl, combine crème fraîche, remaining 2 tablespoons brown sugar and eggs; whisk until creamy. Whisk in flour and salt. Batter will be thin and should be smooth with no lumps. Stir in reserved 2 tablespoons dried plum liquid.

5 Place cooled apples in pastry-lined pan. Pour excess apple syrup from skillet into batter (there should be about 1 tablespoon). Arrange dried plums evenly over apples. Pour batter over fruit. (Batter will come up to top of pastry crust.)

6 Carefully transfer tart onto hot baking sheet in oven. Bake 35 minutes or until puffed, lightly browned and knife inserted in center comes out clean. Cool 20 minutes. Serve warm or at room temperature. Store in refrigerator.

8 servings.

PER SERVING: 580 calories, 38.5 g total fat (15.5 g saturated fat), 6.5 g protein, 54.5 g carbohydrate, 95 mg cholesterol, 230 mg sodium, 3.5 g fiber.

Peach and Blueberry Clafouti Flan

It is not unusual to see a clafouti made with creamy fromage blanc or tangy crème fraîche in France. The result is a dessert like this one, with a heavenly texture, both custardy and soufflé-like.

CLAFOUTI
- ¾ lb. fresh peaches (about 3), peeled, sliced
- ¾ cup fresh blueberries
- 2 (7-oz.) containers crème fraîche
- ½ cup sugar
- 1 teaspoon grated lemon peel
- ½ teaspoon vanilla
- 5 eggs

SAUCE
- ¾ cup apricot preserves
- 3 tablespoons brandy or orange juice

1 Heat oven to 300°F. Fill pan (large enough to hold 9x2-inch round baking dish) with about 1 inch hot water. Place in oven.

2 Arrange peaches in single layer in bottom of 9x2-inch round baking dish. Sprinkle with blueberries.

3 In large bowl, combine crème fraîche and sugar; beat at medium speed until smooth. Add lemon peel, vanilla and 1 of the eggs; beat well. Add remaining 4 eggs; beat until well combined. Reserve 1 cup batter. Pour remaining batter slowly over fruit.

4 Carefully transfer baking dish to water bath in oven. Gently pour reserved batter into baking dish. (Batter will come up almost to top of dish.)

5 Bake 55 to 65 minutes or until custard is slightly puffy, set around edges, yet still jiggly in center. (Small knife inserted in center comes out almost clean with a little custard on it.) Carefully remove from water bath; place on folded towel. Cool 2 hours. Cover with plastic wrap; refrigerate.

6 To prepare sauce, heat preserves in small saucepan over medium-low heat until melted. Stir in brandy. Spoon clafouti onto individual dessert plates. Serve with apricot sauce. Refrigerate leftovers.

8 servings.

PER SERVING: 345 calories, 18.5 g total fat (10.5 g saturated fat), 5.5 g protein, 39 g carbohydrate, 190 mg cholesterol, 70 mg sodium, 1.5 g fiber.

Crème Fraîche

Crème fraîche is a rich, thick cream with a mild, tangy flavor that is similar to sour cream but not as sour. It's used like whipping cream in sauces, soups and desserts such as clafouti. It can be boiled without curdling and whipped to soft peaks. It's sold in the dairy department of grocery stores. You can also make it yourself (check a cookbook for instructions), but plan ahead; it must sit out overnight.

Making Perfect Clafouti

The method for making clafouti is a simple one: Pour a pancake-like batter over fruit in a baking dish. Bake and serve warm or at room temperature, with or without a sauce or topping. Here are some tips for success.

Batter
The typical clafouti batter, usually very thin and creamy, has very few ingredients (some type of cream, eggs, flour and sugar) and is treated similarly to the batter for a crepe or popover. It's traditionally mixed by hand with a balloon wire whisk, but you also can use an electric mixer, blender, food processor or immersion blender.

Clafouti batters often are flavored to add a delicate taste that complements the fruit. You can use vanilla, almond or citrus extracts; grated citrus zest; sweet spices such as cinnamon and cardamom; or a small amount of alcohol or liqueur. Some recipes also call for various creams and cheeses, such as crème fraîche, thick sour cream, fromage blanc, soft goat cheese or mascarpone.

Fruit
The French are adamant about clafouti being the perfect dessert for over-ripe fruit, but you also can use firm, ripe fruit. Apricot and fig halves, delicate peach and nectarine slices, thick slices of plums, kiwi or raw pears, and all berries are beautiful and tasty in a clafouti. For firmer fruits, such as Bosc pears, apples, quince and rhubarb, it's best to either poach them or sauté them briefly in some butter so that the fruit's texture is tender when the clafouti comes out of the oven. Whichever fruit you use, the prepared amount should equal 1½ to 2 cups. If your fruit seems too juicy, drain it well. You can use the excess juice in place of some of the liquid in the batter.

Baking dishes
Clafouti is best baked in a shallow, straight-sided ceramic, porcelain or earthenware baking dish. While the charming scalloped, round ceramic baking dish called a clafouti mold or quiche dish is nice, it is purely optional. Any 9- to 12-inch round or oval baking dish will do, or you can use individual dishes. Use a tart pan with a removable bottom for clafouti with a crust.

If you use a pan that differs from the one called for in a recipe, measure the volume of the pan and use more or less batter as appropriate. Remember to adjust baking times up or down, depending on the size pan you use, and bake until it's golden brown and a knife inserted in the center comes out clean.

You can purchase clafouti pans and other baking dishes in cookware shops or from mail-order sources, such as Williams-Sonoma (877-812-6235; www.williams-sonoma.com), La Cuisine (800-521-1176; www.lacuisineus.com) or Sur La Table (800-243-0852; www.surlatable.com).

Baking
It's important to preheat the baking dish before adding the batter and fruit. (When making clafouti with a crust, this step is eliminated.) The hot dish provides heat quickly, helping the batter puff up while it bakes. For convenience, melt the butter in the baking dish while it heats. Swirl the butter to coat the sides and bottom of the dish before adding the fruit and batter.

Oven temperature
Clafouti should be baked uncovered on the center rack of the oven. It starts baking in a hot oven (425°F). This heats the batter quickly, setting the proteins and turning the liquid into a tender solid, creating an outer crust. After about 10 minutes, the oven temperature is reduced so the clafouti can slowly bake all the way through. This creates a mass of expanding air and steam that is trapped under the outer crust. The result is similar to a soufflé: It has a crusty outer edge and a creamy center. Once it starts cooling, it contracts and falls. That's when it's ready to serve.

The exception to this cooking method is when clafouti is made without flour, such as Peach and Blueberry Clafouti Flan. The custard in this version must be baked at an even, low temperature in a water bath, which moderates the heat even more, to prevent the batter from curdling.

For best flavor and texture, serve clafouti warm, with a simple dusting of powdered sugar or with a fruit sauce, heavy cream, whipped cream or crème fraîche on the side.

Caramel
Crave

Baked Apples with Caramel Sauce

Luscious, golden, homemade caramel is the foundation for delectable autumn desserts.

Text and Recipes by Lisa Saltzman

I t will come as no surprise to those who know me that I am addicted to caramel. Ever since my days as a pastry chef at Chez Panisse in Berkeley, I have been known as the Caramel Queen. Back then, no one could touch my crème caramel. And for the past 10 years, I have made large quantities of my caramel sauce to give as gifts at Christmas.

For me, caramel's versatility makes it the quintessential foundation for desserts. It can be rich and creamy, or light and delicate. And who can resist its glistening amber color?

The technique for making caramel is easy to master. Once learned, you just may become a caramel devotee like me.

Baked Apples with Caramel Sauce

This recipe can be varied by substituting other chopped nuts or dried fruits. Dried currants, cherries or cranberries, and chopped dried apricots, work well, as do pecans, almonds or hazelnuts.

- 6 medium apples (Jonagold, Braeburn or Gala)
- ¼ cup unsalted butter, softened
- ¼ cup packed brown sugar
- 1 teaspoon cinnamon
- ¼ cup pure maple syrup
- ½ cup raisins
- ½ cup finely chopped walnuts
  Creamy Caramel Sauce (recipe follows)

1 Heat oven to 325°F. Remove core from apples with apple corer or small knife; place in 13x9-inch pan.

2 In small bowl, stir together butter, brown sugar, cinnamon and maple syrup. Stir in raisins and walnuts. Spoon mixture into center of apples. Cover with foil.

3 Bake 1 hour to 1 hour 15 minutes or until apples are tender when pierced with knife.

4 Serve apples warm with Creamy Caramel Sauce spooned over top.

6 servings.

PER SERVING: 515 calories, 25 g total fat (12 g saturated fat), 2.5 g protein, 76.5 g carbohydrate, 55 mg cholesterol, 15 mg sodium, 5 g fiber.

Caramel-Cranberry Nut Tart

Caramel-Cranberry Nut Tart

This wonderfully rich tart features a buttery crust and an incredible caramel filling studded with nuts, dried cranberries and chunks of bittersweet chocolate. It is an ideal holiday dessert that can be prepared well in advance and kept refrigerated until ready to serve.

PASTRY
- 1 cup all-purpose flour
- 1 tablespoon sugar
- ¼ teaspoon salt
- ½ cup unsalted butter, cut up, softened
- 2 teaspoons water
- 1 teaspoon vanilla

FILLING
- 1 cup sugar
- 3 tablespoons light corn syrup
- ½ cup unsalted butter, cut up, softened
- ½ cup whipping cream
- ¾ cup coarsely chopped pecans, toasted*
- ¾ cup slivered almonds, toasted*
- ¾ cup dried cranberries

GARNISH
- 2 oz. bittersweet chocolate, coarsely chopped

1 In medium bowl, stir together flour, 1 tablespoon sugar and salt; add ½ cup butter. With pastry blender or 2 knives, cut in butter until

mixture resembles coarse crumbs. In small bowl, combine water and vanilla; add to flour-butter mixture, stirring until dough holds shape when pressed together.

2 Press pastry dough evenly in bottom and up sides of 9-inch tart pan. Place in freezer at least 30 minutes. (Crust can be made up to 4 weeks ahead. Wrap pan in foil and freeze. Do not thaw crust before baking; an additional 5 minutes baking time may be needed.)

3 Heat oven to 375°F. Bake crust, uncovered, 15 minutes. Check crust; if beginning to bubble, gently prick bubbles. Bake an additional 15 to 20 minutes or until crust is golden brown.

4 Remove crust from oven; cool until ready to fill.

5 In heavy medium saucepan, stir together 1 cup sugar and corn syrup. Bring to a boil over medium-high heat. As sugar begins to melt, swirl saucepan gently to combine sugar and syrup. Continue to cook until mixture begins to caramelize. Watch carefully; if necessary, remove saucepan from heat occasionally to stop cooking. When caramel reaches rich golden brown color, remove from heat. Carefully add ½ cup butter and cream. Return to heat; stir until mixture is smooth and butter is melted.

6 Pour caramel into large bowl. Stir in pecans, almonds and cranberries. Pour into baked crust, evenly distributing nuts and berries. Sprinkle chocolate over top. Refrigerate until set, at least 2 hours or up to 8 hours. Serve chilled as caramel will soften at room temperature.

TIP *To toast pecans and almonds, spread on baking sheet; bake at 375°F for 5 to 10 minutes or until light golden brown.

8 servings.

PER SERVING: 640 calories, 43.5 g total fat (19.5 g saturated fat), 5.5 g protein, 63 g carbohydrate, 80 mg cholesterol, 90 mg sodium, 3.5 g fiber.

Pear Upside-Down Cake

A cross between two traditional desserts, tarte Tatin and upside-down cake, this is the ultimate comfort dessert. The pears are lightly poached to avoid excess liquid in the caramel. If desired, good quality canned pear halves also can be used.

PEARS
1½ cups sugar
3 cups water
3 firm but ripe medium pears

CARAMEL
¼ cup unsalted butter, softened
¾ cup sugar

CAKE
½ cup unsalted butter, softened
½ cup sugar

½ teaspoon vanilla
2 eggs
3 egg yolks
⅓ cup all-purpose flour
⅓ cup cornmeal
1¼ teaspoons baking powder
¼ teaspoon salt

1 In large saucepan, bring 1½ cups sugar and 3 cups water to a boil over high heat. Meanwhile, peel, halve and core pears. (Use melon baller to remove core.) Add to sugar syrup. Reduce heat to low; simmer 15 to 20 minutes or until just tender when pierced with small knife, turning once.

2 Gently remove pears from syrup; place on paper towels to drain. Pat dry. Discard syrup.

3 In 9-inch round ovenproof skillet (preferably cast iron)* or cake pan, combine ¼ cup butter and ¾ cup sugar. Cook over medium-high heat, stirring just until butter melts. Mixture will go through several stages before reaching caramel stage. At first, it will look crystallized; then, as it smoothes out, it will look separated. Continue to cook until caramel reaches rich golden brown color, swirling pan if necessary to combine caramel mixture. Remove from heat. Place pear halves, core side up, in circle over caramel.

4 Heat oven to 375°F. In large bowl, beat ½ cup butter and ½ cup sugar at medium speed 5 to 6 minutes or until light and fluffy. Add vanilla. Beat in eggs and egg yolks one at a time, beating well after each addition. In medium bowl, stir together flour, cornmeal, baking powder and salt. Gently stir into butter mixture. Spread batter over pears and caramel.

5 Bake 30 minutes or until toothpick inserted in center comes out clean. Immediately run small knife around sides of cake to loosen. Carefully turn cake upside down onto large round platter. Wait several minutes before removing skillet. (If some of caramel remains in skillet, add 1 tablespoon water; return skillet to medium heat. Cook and stir until caramel melts and forms sauce.

Drizzle over cake.) Serve cake warm with scoop of vanilla ice cream, if desired.

TIP *If ovenproof skillet is not available, use 9x2-inch round cake pan. Make caramel in large saucepan and pour into cake pan.

8 servings.

PER SERVING: 400 calories, 20.5 g total fat (12 g saturated fat), 4 g protein, 52 g carbohydrate, 180 mg cholesterol, 175 mg sodium, 2 g fiber.

Autumn Crème Caramel

The key to a perfect crème caramel is in the baking: Avoid overbaking by removing it from the oven as soon as the custard is set in the center. If bubbles begin to form around the edges, it has gone too far and the custard will be grainy and possibly curdled.

CUSTARD
2½ cups whole milk
½ cup sugar
⅛ teaspoon nutmeg
6 whole cloves
1 small cinnamon stick, broken into 3 pieces
1 (¼-inch) slice fresh ginger, coarsely chopped (½ teaspoon)
3 eggs
3 egg yolks

CARAMEL
¾ cup sugar
¼ cup plus 3 tablespoons water
1½ tablespoons light corn syrup

1 In medium saucepan, stir together milk, ½ cup sugar, nutmeg, cloves, cinnamon and ginger. Slowly bring just to a boil over medium heat. Cover; remove from heat. Let stand 30 minutes.

2 Meanwhile, in heavy medium saucepan, stir together ¾ cup sugar, ¼ cup of the water and corn syrup. Bring to a boil over medium-high heat without stirring. When syrup reaches a boil, swirl pan occasionally to moisten all of sugar. Boil until syrup begins to turn a rich golden brown color. Remove from heat; carefully add 3 tablespoons water to caramel. Place over medium heat; cook until hardened caramel dissolves, stirring constantly. Pour caramel into 6 (4-oz.) ramekins or custard cups, swirling cups to line with caramel. Place ramekins in large baking pan.

3 Heat oven to 350°F. In medium bowl, whisk together eggs and egg yolks. Bring milk mixture to a boil over medium heat. Gradually add hot milk mixture to eggs, whisking constantly. Strain custard through fine strainer.

4 Pour into ramekins. Carefully pour hot tap water into baking pan so it comes halfway up sides of ramekins. Cover pan tightly with foil.

5 Bake 30 minutes or until custards are set but still wobble when tapped. Remove ramekins from baking pan; refrigerate until cold.

6 To unmold, run small knife around inside edge of each ramekin; invert onto plate.

6 servings.

PER SERVING: 305 calories, 8.5 g total fat (3.5 g saturated fat), 8 g protein, 50.5 g carbohydrate, 225 mg cholesterol, 90 mg sodium, 0 g fiber.

Creamy Caramel Sauce

Not only is this caramel sauce a wonderful accompaniment to a variety of desserts, it also can be made in large quantities to give as a delicious food gift.

- ¼ **cup water**
- 1 **cup sugar**
- ¼ **cup unsalted butter, cut up**
- ½ **cup whipping cream**

1 In medium saucepan, combine water and sugar; stir until all sugar is moistened. Bring to a boil over medium-high heat. Cook until syrup is rich golden brown color. Do not stir during cooking as mixture can easily crystallize. To test for correct color, using spoon, drop small amount of caramel onto white paper or plate. Color should not be light or caramel sauce will be pale.

2 When caramel reaches desired color, remove from heat. Carefully add butter and cream. Bring to a boil over medium heat, stirring until hardened caramel dissolves and sauce is smooth.

3 Serve warm with baked apples, or as sauce with ice cream, apple pie or other desserts. Store in refrigerator; reheat before using.

1 cup.

PER 2 TABLESPOONS: 190 calories, 10.5 g total fat (6.5 g saturated fat), .5 g protein, 25.5 g carbohydrate, 30 mg cholesterol, 5 mg sodium, 0 g fiber.

Making Creamy, Smooth Caramel

Two Methods

Dry method In this method, the sugar is melted in a pan without any additional ingredients. As the sugar cooks, it melts and creates a thick syrup that, when boiled, reaches the caramel stage. This method requires close attention because the sugar can clump and melt unevenly and possibly burn, giving the caramel a bitter flavor.

Wet method The sugar is combined with water or another liquid, creating a thin sugar syrup. During the boiling process, the excess liquid evaporates, causing the syrup to thicken, the sugar concentration to increase and the color to change from an opaque white to a rich golden brown. This method takes a little longer but is easier to control and therefore is better for beginners.

Avoiding Problems

When making caramel, there is the danger of crystallization—the formation of sugar crystals that can interfere with the syrup's texture. If the pan or spoon is not completely clean, if the syrup is stirred once it boils, or if the sugar is not properly dissolved, crystallization can take place. To avoid this problem, make the caramel in a smooth, clean pan. As the sugar begins to melt, brush away any sugar crystals that cling to the side of the pan by using a pastry brush dipped in water or by covering the pan briefly to allow the steam to wash away any sugar crystals on the side of the pan. Acid also interferes with crystallization, so ½ teaspoon of lemon juice, white vinegar or cream of tartar can be added to the sugar mixture to prevent crystallization.

In the wet method, combine the sugar and water or other ingredients in a heavy pan over medium heat. Stir just until the sugar is dissolved. In the dry method, wait for the sugar to melt before stirring. For either method, make sure the sugar is completely dissolved before bringing it to a boil. Bring to a boil over medium to medium-high heat. Once boiling, swirl the pan occasionally to combine the ingredients, but do not stir.

When the syrup begins to turn a light gold color, watch carefully. You may want to take the pan off the heat for a minute to slow down the cooking—the heat of the pan will continue to cook the caramel and you will be able to control the heat. To test for the proper color, take a spoonful of the syrup from the pan and pour it onto a white plate or paper. The color should be rich golden brown. A candy thermometer can be used (cook the syrup to 340°F to 350°F), but it is easier to control caramel just by watching the color. To stop the cooking, remove the pan from the heat and plunge it into a bowl of cold water, making sure the water does not come in contact with the caramel.

Complete Stories

Feature ingredients, wonderful creations.

Blue
Streak

(Left to Right) Maytag Blue, Great Hill Blue, Jersey Blue

An expanding field of worthy contenders puts American blue cheese on the map—and in the kitchen.

Text and Recipes by Laura Werlin

Cheesemaking in America today is no less of a gastronomic revolution than American winemaking was in the 1970s. In just a decade, an industry that began with a handful of specialty cheesemakers has grown into several hundred producers. Among them are cheesemakers who have taken on the difficult-to-make blue cheeses and turned them into sought-after treasures.

As a category, blue cheese simply refers to its mark of distinction: blue veins. These veins are created by the combination of a specific mold and air. The cheeses vary in taste, depending on how they are made. Some blues have a creamy texture, others are crumbly, and still others have a cheddar-like consistency. The color of the veins also varies, from bluish-green to grayish-blue, or even purple or black. Likewise, the amount of salt the cheesemaker uses differs.

The most famous American blue cheese is Iowa's Maytag Blue, but others, such as Wisconsin's BelGioioso Gorgonzola and Massachusetts' Great Hill Blue, are becoming part of the vernacular of American blue cheese aficionados.

Blue cheese gets high marks in the kitchen, too. It adds an earthy richness to a variety of dishes. Its texture turns a pasta silken, while its flavor elevates a simple pork chop to elegance.

Crispy Chicken Salad with Blue Cheese and Spinach

This dish provides the perfect transition from winter to spring. The warm chicken breasts pay homage to the still-cool weather, but the fresh greens underneath are symbolic of the forthcoming spring. Of course, you can make and enjoy this at any time of the year or when you come upon your favorite blue cheese in the store or at the farmers' market. You can use any type of blue cheese you like for this dish; it's simply a matter of personal taste. Try a creamy yet crumbly mild blue, such as Maytag Blue or Great Hill Blue.

- 4 boneless skinless chicken breast halves
- ½ cup panko (Japanese-style bread crumbs)*
- 2 tablespoons finely grated Parmesan cheese
- ½ teaspoon kosher (coarse) salt
- ½ teaspoon freshly ground pepper
- 1 egg
- 5 tablespoons olive oil
- 1 tablespoon unsalted butter
- 1 cup (4 oz.) crumbled blue cheese
- 3 tablespoons balsamic vinegar
- 8 cups baby spinach

1 Heat oven to 400°F. With meat pounder or smooth side of meat mallet, pound chicken breast halves to ½-inch thickness. In shallow bowl, combine panko, Parmesan cheese, ¼ teaspoon of the salt and ¼ teaspoon of the pepper; mix well. Beat egg in another shallow bowl. Dip chicken in egg; coat with bread crumb mixture. Place chicken on plate.

2 In large skillet, heat 2 tablespoons of the oil and the butter over medium-high heat until butter is melted and begins to sizzle. Add chicken; cook 4 to 5 minutes or until golden brown and no longer pink in center, turning once. Place chicken on baking sheet; top with ½ cup of the blue cheese.

3 Bake 5 minutes or until cheese is melted. Transfer chicken to cutting board; cool slightly while preparing salad.

4 In small bowl, whisk together vinegar and remaining ¼ teaspoon salt and pepper; slowly whisk in remaining 3 tablespoons oil. In large bowl, toss together spinach, remaining ½ cup blue cheese and balsamic dressing; mix well.

5 To serve, place salad on individual plates. Cut chicken into ½-inch slices. Fan slices over salad.

TIP *Panko are coarse bread crumbs usually found next to other bread crumbs in the supermarket.

4 servings.

PER SERVING: 510 calories, 34 g total fat (11.5 g saturated fat), 39 g protein, 13 g carbohydrate, 135 mg cholesterol, 835 mg sodium, 3.5 g fiber.

Spicy Orecchiette with Broccoli, White Beans, Leeks and Blue Cheese

Although this is an all-vegetable dish, it is hearty because of the combination of pasta and beans. Add to that the earthy blue cheese, and you have a dish that falls neatly into the category of comfort food. Use a creamy, slightly salty cheese such as Great Hill Blue. It is important to note that this recipe calls for undercooking the broccoli. Resist the temptation to cook it through, or you'll end up with soggy vegetables. The broccoli will reach its doneness in the final cooking stage.

- 12 oz. orecchiette (small disk-shaped pasta), farfalle or shell-shaped pasta
- 1 tablespoon olive oil
- 2 leeks (white and light green parts only), coarsely chopped
- 3 large garlic cloves, minced
- 6 cups broccoli florets (about ¾ lb.)
- 1 cup reduced-sodium vegetable broth or chicken broth
- 1 (15-oz.) can great Northern beans, undrained
- ½ teaspoon kosher (coarse) salt
- 1 teaspoon crushed red pepper
- ¼ teaspoon freshly ground black pepper
- 1½ cups (6 oz.) crumbled blue cheese

1 Cook orecchiette in large pot of boiling salted water according to package directions.

2 Meanwhile, heat oil in large skillet over medium-high heat until hot. Add leeks; cook 4 to 5 minutes or until wilted but not brown. Add garlic; cook 1 minute. Add broccoli and broth. Cover; bring to a boil. Cook 2 to 3 minutes or until broccoli is crisp-tender. Add undrained beans, salt, crushed red pepper and black pepper; stir gently. Cook 1 to 2 minutes or until beans are heated.

3 Reserve ½ cup pasta cooking water. Drain pasta; return to pot. Add broccoli mixture. Increase heat to medium-high; add ¼ cup of the pasta water. Bring to a boil. Add 1 cup of the cheese; stir until cheese is melted and hot. Add additional ¼ cup pasta water if necessary to thin sauce. Serve sprinkled with remaining ½ cup cheese.

4 (1¾-cup) servings.

PER SERVING: 670 calories, 18 g total fat (9 g saturated fat), 31.5 g protein, 97.5 g carbohydrate, 30 mg cholesterol, 1240 mg sodium, 12 g fiber.

Butternut Squash, Sage and Blue Cheese Gratin

The bright orange color of the squash peeking out from beneath the blanket of melted cheese is enough to make you want to dig right into this gratin. Use a semi-firm Stiltonlike blue cheese, such as Blythedale Farm's Jersey Blue or Bingham Hill's Rustic Blue. You may assemble this easy-to-make gratin as much as six hours in advance and refrigerate it. Bring it to room temperature before baking.

- 1 butternut squash (about 1¾ lbs.)
- 1 tablespoon olive oil
- 1 tablespoon chopped fresh sage
- ¼ teaspoon kosher (coarse) salt
- ¼ teaspoon freshly ground pepper
- ¾ cup (3 oz.) crumbled blue cheese
- ¼ cup (1 oz.) shredded Gruyère cheese

1 Heat oven to 375°F. Spray 11x7½-inch baking dish with nonstick cooking spray.

2 Cut squash in half lengthwise; remove seeds and peel. Slice each half crosswise into ½-inch-thick slices. Place squash in single layer at 45-degree angle in baking dish. (The squash will be tightly packed.)

3 Drizzle squash with oil. Sprinkle with sage, salt and pepper. Cover with foil.

4 Bake 40 minutes or until squash is tender. Remove from oven; remove foil. Sprinkle with blue cheese and Gruyère cheese. Return to oven; bake an additional 1 minute or until cheese is melted.

6 servings.

PER SERVING: 150 calories, 8 g total fat (4 g saturated fat), 5.5 g protein, 17 g carbohydrate, 15 mg cholesterol, 280 mg sodium, 3.5 g fiber.

Pork Chops with Blue Cheese, Port-Soaked Figs and Caramelized Onions

Figs and blue cheese are a classic combination. When they become the filling for pork chops, they provide a lovely sweet and salty "seasoning" for the mild meat. Use a creamy Gorgonzola such as BelGioioso.

- 2 tablespoons olive oil
- 1 large red onion (about 1 lb.), thinly sliced
- ½ teaspoon kosher (coarse) salt
- ¼ teaspoon freshly ground pepper
- 2 cups port or red wine
- 1 cup chopped dried figs
- 1 bay leaf
- ¾ cup (3 oz.) crumbled Gorgonzola cheese
- 4 (6- to 8-oz.) bone-in pork loin chops

Spicy Orecchiette with
Broccoli, White Beans, Leeks
and Blue Cheese

Pork Chops with Blue Cheese,
Port-Soaked Figs and Caramelized Onions

1 Heat 1 tablespoon of the oil in large ovenproof skillet over medium heat until hot. Reduce heat to medium-low. Add onion; cook 20 to 30 minutes or until onion is golden brown, stirring frequently. (Be patient because the longer the onion cooks, the sweeter it becomes.)

2 Stir in ¼ teaspoon of the salt and ⅛ teaspoon of the pepper. Place onion in medium bowl; set aside. Reserve unwashed skillet. (Onion may become slightly gray in color as it stands. This will not affect the sauce.)

3 Meanwhile, in medium saucepan, bring port, figs and bay leaf to a boil over medium-high heat. Boil 1 minute. Remove from heat; cover and let stand 20 minutes. Drain figs, reserving figs and port; discard bay leaf. Place figs in small bowl; cool to room temperature. Stir in cheese.

4 Heat oven to 400°F. Slice each pork chop horizontally to form

pocket. Spoon fig mixture into each pocket, pressing filling in firmly. Press pork together to enclose filling. Place remaining 1 tablespoon oil in reserved skillet. Place pork chops in skillet; turn to coat with oil. Sprinkle chops with remaining ¼ teaspoon salt and ⅛ teaspoon pepper.

5 Bake 15 to 20 minutes or until pork chops are golden brown and no longer pink in center, turning once. Remove from skillet; place on serving platter. Cover loosely with foil.

6 To make sauce, heat same skillet (with drippings) over medium-high heat until hot. Add reserved port and onion; bring to a boil, stirring to scrape up browned bits from bottom of skillet. Boil until reduced by half, about 5 minutes. Spoon onion and port over pork chops.

4 servings.

PER SERVING: 610 calories, 28.5 g total fat (10.5 g saturated fat), 35.5 g protein, 56 g carbohydrate, 95 mg cholesterol, 555 mg sodium, 6.5 g fiber.

Making and Storing Blue Cheese

How it's made

Cheesemaking is the delicate balance between science and art. The science involves elements such as milk temperature, the bacteria and rennet used, salting, aging and timing. The art is in the hands of the cheesemaker, who decides how these elements should be combined.

When it comes to making blue cheese, the basic method is no different. However, it becomes a blue cheese because of two essential steps: First, a mold is added to the milk to set the stage for the eventual blue cheese flavor as well as the bluing process. Second, as blue cheese is aged, the cheesemaker literally skewers the cheese to allow oxygen to enter the center of the cheese. When the oxygen combines with the molds already in the cheese, the blue veins are formed. Some cheeses, such as Gorgonzola, don't require the second step. Because the curds are loosely packed, there is already oxygen circulating around them, and the blue veining occurs on its own.

The process for making blue cheese naturally results in different flavors and textures, even though such cheeses are often grouped under the generic category of blue cheese. Gorgonzola tends to have greenish veins and is usually a little softer. A Stiltonlike cheese is much more yellow, has more extensive greenish-blue veining and becomes fairly crumbly with age. Some soft blue cheeses can be almost like Brie in texture, and a cheese such as Maytag Blue can be distinguished because the cheese is mostly creamy white, except for occasional blue specks or marbling throughout the cheese.

How to store

Storing blue cheese involves striking the delicate balance between providing enough air for the cheese to breathe, yet enough moisture to prevent the cheese from drying out. As a general rule, storing any type of cheese in waxed or parchment paper in the cheese or produce drawer of the refrigerator is usually best. Both papers keep most of the air out, providing a nice, humid environment for the cheese; yet both also allow a bit of air to penetrate the cheese, keeping the dryness-moisture ratio in balance.

Because blue cheeses vary in moisture, the way to store them depends on the style of the cheese. If the blue cheese is quite creamy and soft, store it in an airtight plastic container with a few pinholes. This retains a humid environment to keep the cheese creamy, yet provides enough air to keep it from going bad. For semisoft to semihard blue cheese, wrap the cheese in waxed or parchment paper. Don't use plastic wrap; it tends to trap humidity, creating a moldy cheese. The wrap should be changed every two days or every time you use the cheese, whichever is more frequent. This staves off mold.

American Cheesemakers Focus on Blue

More and more American cheesemakers are turning to blue. Because cheesemakers know no geographical boundaries in the United States, excellent blues are being made from coast to coast.

Jersey Blue

In Corinth, Vermont, Blythedale Farm has been making blue cheese from the milk of its 20 Jersey cows for about two years. Called Jersey Blue, it's a Stilton-like cheese with lots of blue veining and a rich golden color that is the hallmark of Jersey milk. It's a raw milk cheese and is aged five months, resulting in a thin crust-like brownish rind and significant veining, yet a relative mildness that belies its appearance. Because just two people, Karen Galayda and Tom Gilbert, run the entire operation, which includes production of Brie, Camembert, Gruyère and a Parmesan-like cheese, all of their cheeses are made in relatively small quantities.

Vermont Blue

Farther north in Highgate Center, Vermont, Dawn and Dan Boucher are relative newcomers to cheesemaking. They have had a Holstein milk dairy, Boucher Family Farm, for some time but added cheesemaking in 1999. They set their sights exclusively on blue-veined cheeses, and six months out of the gate, their Vermont Blue, made under the Green Mountain Blue Cheese label, was an award winner at the 1999 American Cheese Society competition. This rindless raw milk cheese is aged for four months, and, because the curds are loosely packed, the air circulates throughout the cheese to create extensive veining. Their other blue cheeses include a Gorgonzola that is aged for one year, and Wild Blue, a slightly creamier cheese with less veining but no less of the earthy blue flavor.

Great Hill Blue

In Marion, Massachusetts, Tim Stone of Great Hill Dairy has also been making blue cheese exclusively since he began to make cheese in 1996. In 1999, his Great Hill Blue was given a much-deserved blue ribbon by the American Cheese Society, and it has quickly become the standard of American blues. Great Hill Blue is unique because it's made with nonhomogenized milk, which has larger fat globules. Stone says this creates the rich flavor and creamy texture of his cheese. His cheese has a fair amount of salt and blue-green veins, which are created by the air that enters the cheese when holes are pierced in it once it begins to age. About 12 months later, the cheese is ready.

Rustic Blue

They call their cheese Rustic Blue, but the owners of Bingham Hill Cheese Company in Fort Collins, Colorado, have made a cheese that is far more elegant than its name suggests. As relative new-comers to the American cheese-making scene, Tom and Kristi Johnson have already established a stellar reputation for their blue cheese, which is reminiscent of Stilton cheese. In fact, their cheese took first place in the blue cheese category at the 2000 American Cheese Society Conference. Rustic Blue is unpasteurized; it's a fairly solid cheese that can be cut into slices, shaved or broken into shards. It has a creamy, slightly sweet taste balanced by a fair amount of salt and rich, earthy notes from the grayish-blue veins. The rind is a pinkish-gray, which, unlike Stilton, is edible.

BelGioioso Gorgonzola

Wisconsin is the site of one of America's best-made Gorgonzola cheeses. At BelGioioso Cheese, it's made on a larger scale than many American cheeses. The company began as an Italian company's American branch. Eventually Errico Auricchio, who was sent from Italy to start the factory, bought the American enterprise from his family, and he's been making Italian-style cheeses ever since. The Gorgonzola is a wonderful study in creaminess, as Auricchio is a stickler for perfectly ripened Gorgonzola. He does not like it too dry, which he often finds in Italian Gorgonzolas. He says this dryness is the result of the Italian Gorgonzolas often staying too long in transit from Europe to the United States.

Maytag Blue

The Grande Dame of blue cheeses is Maytag Blue, made in Iowa. It is not simply longevity that has kept the reputation of this cheese alive; it is unsurpassed quality. Maytag Blue continues to be made much the way it began in the mid-1940s, and Maytag Dairy Farms' current CEO, Jim Stevens, had a big hand in what we eat today. Stevens has been with Maytag nearly from the beginning, and shortly after joining the company became its cheesemaker. His talent led to the wonderfully balanced cheese —not too strong, not too mild—that has an unmistakable blue cheese flavor, offset by its creaminess. The cheese is cave-ripened, just as it has been since the beginning, and it is made with unpasteurized milk. It's aged at least two months and often much longer.

Roast Chicken with Baby Beets, Asparagus and Potatoes

Chicken and vegetables come together in a medley of seasonal dishes.

Text and Recipes by Kathleen Prisant

It's not just the weather that turns mild this time of year. As tender spring vegetables and herbs begin to appear in markets, winter cravings for bold, spicy dishes give way to quieter longings. Spring produce begs for simpler, more delicate preparations—and pleasant, harmonious partners. That's where chicken comes in. Paired with asparagus, baby beets, fresh herbs and other young newcomers, mild-mannered poultry is transformed into a light, heavenly scented supper.

These recipes offer a medley of ways to prepare chicken, from sautéing and roasting to grilling and poaching, each with palate-pleasing results. Give in to your cravings and take a culinary walk on the mild side.

Roast Chicken with Baby Beets, Asparagus and Potatoes

Olive oil infused with garlic and fennel does double duty as a baste for roasting and as a sauce added just before serving. Crushing the fennel and garlic helps to release their flavors into the oil.

- 1½ teaspoons fennel seeds
- ¼ cup olive oil
- 2 large garlic cloves, finely chopped
- ½ teaspoon salt
- 1 (3½-lb.) cut-up chicken, large breasts halved
- 12 fingerling potatoes or small red potatoes, halved
- 12 baby beets, peeled
- 1 lb. asparagus
- 3 tablespoons balsamic vinegar

1 Heat oven to 400°F. Toast fennel seeds in small dry skillet over medium heat 30 to 60 seconds or until fragrant, stirring constantly. Cool. Crush seeds with mortar and pestle or with side of chef's knife. Return to skillet; add oil and garlic. Heat over low heat until oil is hot. Remove from heat. Cover; let stand 15 minutes. Stir in salt.

2 Line 17x12x1-inch pan with foil. Arrange chicken, potatoes and beets in pan. Drizzle with 2 tablespoons of the oil mixture. Bake 20 minutes.

3 Remove from oven; stir vegetables. Add asparagus; drizzle with 1 tablespoon of the oil mixture. Return to oven; bake an additional 25 to 30 minutes or until vegetables are tender and chicken juices run clear. If vegetables are done before chicken, remove vegetables and

Chicken in Herb Pesto Broth

continue cooking chicken 10 to 15 minutes or until done.

4 Place chicken and vegetables on platter. Stir vinegar into remaining oil mixture; drizzle over chicken and vegetables.

6 servings.

PER SERVING: 385 calories, 16.5 g total fat (3 g saturated fat), 31.5 g protein, 29.5 g carbohydrate, 80 mg cholesterol, 325 mg sodium, 4.5 g fiber.

Spring Chicken Soup

This delicate soup features a trio of green vegetables: peas, green beans and zucchini. Fresh fava beans also would make a nice addition. If you like, substitute them for the peas. Shell the beans, then add them to boiling water for 1 minute; drain and rinse with cold water. Remove the outer skin of each bean by pinching the end; the bean will slide out. Add them as you would the peas.

- 1 teaspoon fennel seeds
- ¼ teaspoon cumin seeds
- 1 (1-inch) piece fresh ginger
- 2 large garlic cloves
- 4 sprigs fresh thyme
- 8 cups reduced-sodium chicken broth
- 3 boneless skinless chicken breast halves, sliced diagonally (⅜ inch)
- 1 cup fresh or frozen baby peas
- 1 cup sliced (1 inch) green beans
- 1 cup julienned zucchini
- ½ teaspoon salt

1 Toast fennel seeds and cumin seeds in small dry skillet over medium heat 30 to 60 seconds or until fragrant, stirring constantly.

2 With side of chef's knife or cleaver, gently smash ginger and garlic. In center of 8-inch square of cheesecloth, place ginger, garlic, thyme, fennel seeds and cumin seeds. Tie with kitchen string.

3 Place chicken broth in large saucepan or Dutch oven. Add cheesecloth bag. Bring to a boil over high heat. Reduce heat to medium; cook 15 minutes.

4 Add chicken, peas, green beans, zucchini and salt. Return to a boil over high heat. Reduce heat to medium-low; simmer 5 to 8 minutes or until chicken is no longer pink in center and vegetables are crisp-tender. Remove and discard cheesecloth bag.

6 servings.

PER SERVING: 150 calories, 4 g total fat (1 g saturated fat), 21.5 g protein, 6 g carbohydrate, 35 mg cholesterol, 895 mg sodium, 2 g fiber.

Chicken in Herb Pesto Broth

Chicken breasts are surrounded by a lovely garlic-herb broth laced with vegetables. This dish is not really a soup; there's just enough broth to line a deep plate or shallow bowl.

PESTO
- 2 medium garlic cloves, chopped
- ½ cup chopped fresh Italian parsley
- ½ cup chopped fresh chives
- ¼ cup chopped fresh thyme
- ¼ cup olive oil
- 2 teaspoons lemon juice
- ½ teaspoon salt

CHICKEN AND VEGETABLES
- 1 tablespoon olive oil
- 6 boneless skinless chicken breast halves
- 2 cups reduced-sodium chicken broth
- ½ cup diced carrot (¼ inch)
- 1 cup fresh or frozen corn
- ½ cup fresh or frozen peas

1 In blender, combine all pesto ingredients; blend until smooth.

2 Heat 1 tablespoon oil in large skillet over medium-high heat until hot. Add chicken; cook 3 to 4 minutes or until brown, turning once. Reduce heat to medium-low; cover and continue cooking 7 to 10 minutes or until juices run clear. Slice chicken diagonally into ½-inch strips.

3 Meanwhile, bring broth to a boil in medium saucepan over medium-high heat. Add carrot; cook 2 minutes. Add corn and peas; cook an additional 2 minutes or until vegetables are crisp-tender. Whisk in pesto.

4 To serve, ladle generous ⅓ cup broth and vegetables into each plate or bowl. Top with sliced chicken.

6 servings.

PER SERVING: 300 calories, 16 g total fat (3 g saturated fat), 30 g protein, 9 g carbohydrate, 75 mg cholesterol, 440 mg sodium, 2 g fiber.

Grilled Kabobs with Two Layers of Flavor

Grilling sauces can burn easily if they are brushed over the food too early in the cooking process. Such a problem is avoided here by marinating the chicken in a flavorful mixture that gets a kick from hot chili oil, then glazing all the ingredients with hoisin sauce during the last half of the cooking time.

- 3 tablespoons soy sauce
- 2 tablespoons lime juice
- 1 teaspoon hot chili oil
- 1 teaspoon grated fresh ginger
- 1¼ lb. boneless skinless chicken thighs, cut into 1½-inch pieces
- 2 zucchini (or 1 zucchini and 1 yellow summer squash), cut into 1-inch pieces
- 1 Japanese eggplant, cut into 1-inch pieces
- 12 small button mushrooms
- 1 tablespoon vegetable oil
- ⅓ cup hoisin sauce
- ½ teaspoon five-spice powder*

1 In small bowl, combine soy sauce, lime juice, chili oil and ginger. Stir in chicken. Let stand at room temperature 20 minutes to marinate.

2 Meanwhile, in medium bowl, combine zucchini, eggplant and mushrooms; toss with oil.

3 Heat grill. Thread chicken, zucchini, eggplant and mushrooms onto 6 (12-inch) metal skewers; discard marinade.

4 Place kabobs on gas grill over medium heat or on charcoal grill 4 to 6 inches from medium coals. Cook 3 to 5 minutes, turning once. Meanwhile, in small bowl, mix hoisin sauce and five-spice powder.

5 Remove from grill. Brush kabobs

Lemon Chicken Salad

with hoisin mixture. Return to grill; cook an additional 2 to 3 minutes or until chicken is no longer pink in center and vegetables are tender, turning once.

TIP *Five-spice powder is a prepared seasoning that often includes star anise, cloves, cinnamon, fennel seed and pepper. It can be found in the spice or Asian foods section of the grocery store.

6 servings.

PER SERVING: 235 calories, 11 g total fat (3 g saturated fat), 22.5 g protein, 12.5 g carbohydrate, 60 mg cholesterol, 400 mg sodium, 3 g fiber.

Lemon Chicken Salad

Poaching is a great way to cook chicken for a salad. Here, the vinaigrette penetrates the chicken most effectively if it's added while the chicken is still warm. For a more pronounced lemon flavor, let the chicken marinate longer.

VINAIGRETTE
2½ tablespoons lemon juice
2 teaspoons grated lemon peel
½ teaspoon Dijon mustard
¾ teaspoon ground cardamom
½ teaspoon ground coriander
½ teaspoon salt
¼ teaspoon ground cumin
⅓ cup olive oil

SALAD
1 whole poached chicken, skin removed, meat shredded (about 3½ cups)
12 asparagus spears, cut into 2-inch pieces
1 large or 3 baby gold or red beets, peeled, thinly sliced with vegetable peeler
½ small red onion, cut into thin wedges
6 cups mixed spring salad greens

1 In small bowl, whisk together all vinaigrette ingredients.

2 Toss half of dressing with chicken. Cover; refrigerate at least 2 hours or until serving time.

3 In medium saucepan, cook asparagus in boiling salted water 3 to 4 minutes or until crisp-tender. Drain; rinse with cold water to cool.

4 In large bowl, toss asparagus, beets, onion and salad greens. Drizzle with remaining dressing; stir gently to coat. Arrange on serving platter. Top with chicken.

6 servings.

PER SERVING: 285 calories, 18.5 g total fat (3.5 g saturated fat), 25.5 g protein, 5.5 g carbohydrate, 70 mg cholesterol, 295 mg sodium, 2 g fiber.

Poaching Chicken

This method of poaching chicken results in tender and succulent meat that's perfect for salads, shredded chicken salad sandwiches, soups, tortilla fillings, frittatas and more. Save the stock for soups or sauces.

Poached Whole Chicken

1 (3½-lb.) whole chicken
2 sprigs fresh thyme
1 sprig fresh parsley
1 bay leaf
1 rib celery, halved crosswise
Water, as needed to cover chicken

1 Place chicken in large pot or Dutch oven. Place thyme, parsley and bay leaf in hollow of one half of celery rib; cover with other half celery rib. With kitchen string, tie to form bundle. Place in pot.

2 Add water to cover. Cover; place over medium-high heat. Bring to a boil. Reduce heat to medium-low or low; simmer 25 to 30 minutes or until chicken juices run clear and internal temperature reaches 175°F to 180°F.

3 Cool until easy to handle. Remove skin and shred chicken; refrigerate until ready to use.

4 Remove celery bundle from stock; discard. Simmer stock until reduced to 4 cups. Strain through fine mesh strainer or cheesecloth. Refrigerate, uncovered, until cold. Cover; refrigerate up to 3 days or freeze until ready to use.

6 servings; 3½ cups shredded chicken and about 4 cups stock

PER SERVING: 150 calories, 5 g total fat (1.5 g saturated fat), 23.5 g protein, 0 g carbohydrate, 70 mg cholesterol, 65 mg sodium, 0 g fiber.

Coco Loco Brûlée

Coconuts take the lead roles in a summertime menu brimming with flavor.

Text and Recipes by Steven Raichlen

There was a time in the United States when coconut was available in just one form: the sweetened dried stuff sprinkled on cupcakes. How times have changed! The heightened interest in exotic foods and the popularity of Latin cuisine have brought coconut to American kitchens in many forms. Coconut water makes a refreshing beverage, and coconut meat is a comforting snack as well as a versatile ingredient for many types of dishes. Coconut milk behaves just like heavy cream, while coconut cream is indispensable to the bartender.

Fresh coconut is eaten when it's young and soft as well as when it's hard and mature. It's also enjoyed as a beverage, and it can be dried. Fresh or dried coconut can be used as an ingredient in any number of dishes, from soups and appetizers to stir-fries and desserts.

If your experience with coconut has been limited, it's time you discovered the treasure that lies beneath its rugged exterior. You'll be sweetly rewarded.

Coco Loco Brûlée

You don't have to serve this divine coconut crème brûlée in a coconut shell, but it sure makes it fun! The custard is first cooked in a rectangular baking dish. Then, when you're ready to serve it, spoon the custard into the coconut halves, sprinkle with sugar and caramelize the sugar.

    2 cups whipping cream
    1 cup coconut milk
    1 cup cream of coconut
    1 vanilla bean, halved lengthwise
    1 cup sugar
   10 egg yolks
    4 coconuts

1 Heat oven to 325°F. Place 13x9-inch glass baking dish in shallow roasting pan.

2 In large heavy saucepan, combine cream, coconut milk, cream of coconut and vanilla bean. Bring to a boil over medium heat; remove from heat.

3 Meanwhile, whisk ½ cup of the sugar and egg yolks in large bowl until smooth. Slowly whisk in hot cream mixture. Strain through fine sieve into baking dish. Pour ½ inch hot water into roasting pan to create water bath.

4 Place roasting pan with baking dish in oven. Bake 25 to 35 minutes or until just barely set but still quivery. Do not overbake. Remove from water bath. Cool to room temperature. Refrigerate until cold. (Custard can be made up to 1 day ahead. Cover and refrigerate.)

5 Meanwhile, crack coconuts in half with hammer (see pg. 147); reserve coconut water, if desired. Just before

Brazilian Coconut Tuna

serving, spoon custard into coconut halves. Smooth top of mixture with back of spoon. Sprinkle 1 tablespoon of the remaining sugar in thin layer over filling in each coconut. With blowtorch,* caramelize sugar. Serve in shallow bowls.

TIP *Mini blowtorches are used by pastry chefs and cooks. They can be found in department stores and gourmet kitchen shops. A regular blowtorch also can be used.

8 servings.

PER SERVING: 480 calories, 38.5 g total fat (26 g saturated fat), 6 g protein, 31 g carbohydrate, 330 mg cholesterol, 40 mg sodium, 0 g fiber.

Brazilian Coconut Tuna

Fish steaks have a tendency to dry out when grilled. That's why this coconut marinade—redolent with garlic and peppers—is so perfectly suited to tuna. The high-fat content of the coconut milk keeps the fish moist and flavorful. Serve the tuna with Coconut-Pineapple Rice.

1 medium onion, coarsely chopped
½ green bell pepper, coarsely chopped
½ red bell pepper, coarsely chopped

5 medium garlic cloves, coarsely chopped
1 cup coconut milk
2 tablespoons olive oil
¼ cup coarsely chopped fresh cilantro
1 teaspoon salt
1 teaspoon freshly ground black pepper
4 (6-oz.) tuna steaks

1 In food processor, combine onion, green bell pepper, red bell pepper and garlic; process until finely chopped. Add coconut milk, oil, cilantro, salt and black pepper; process until well blended.

2 Pour ⅓ of marinade into baking dish. Arrange tuna steaks in dish. Pour remaining marinade over fish. Refrigerate 4 to 6 hours to marinate, turning fish several times.

3 Heat grill. Lightly oil grill; place fish on gas grill over medium heat or on charcoal grill 4 to 6 inches from medium coals. Cook 4 to 6 minutes for medium-rare, turning once.

4 servings.

PER SERVING: 265 calories, 13 g total fat (5 g saturated fat), 33 g protein, 2.5 g carbohydrate, 100 mg cholesterol, 245 mg sodium, .5 g fiber.

Coconut Beef Saté with Peanut Sauce

This saté comes from Indonesia. What makes the dish so unique and flavorful is the addition of shredded coconut to the beef. To be strictly authentic, you'd use kejap manis, a sweet Indonesian soy sauce. Look for it at an Asian market, or use equal parts regular soy sauce and molasses, as called for in the recipe.

- ¾ lb. lean ground beef
- 1 cup shredded coconut (dried or fresh, sweetened or unsweetened)
- 2 teaspoons minced fresh ginger
- 1 teaspoon minced garlic
- ½ teaspoon salt
- ½ teaspoon ground turmeric
- ½ teaspoon ground coriander
- ½ teaspoon freshly ground pepper
- 1 tablespoon molasses
- 1 tablespoon soy sauce
- 1 teaspoon fresh lime juice Peanut Sauce (recipe follows)

1 In large bowl, combine all ingredients except Peanut Sauce; mix with hands or large spoon until well blended.

2 For each saté, shape 1 tablespoon beef mixture around 1 (8-inch) bamboo skewer, making saté 4 inches long. Place on ungreased baking sheet. (Satés can be prepared up to 3 hours ahead. Cover and refrigerate.)

3 Heat grill. Cut large sheet of heavy-duty foil; fold in half to make

Coconut Know-How

What most of us call coconut—a hard sphere 4 to 5 inches in diameter covered with a shaggy brown shell—is actually the core of the nut. The edible part is the ½-inch layer of white flesh underneath the shell. It wasn't until I visited the Bahamas that I encountered the coconut in its natural state: a large, green, oblong fruit weighing 5 to 6 pounds, encased in a fibrous husk. As I lounged on the beach, an itinerant vendor prepared one of these behemoths for me, whacking the top off with a machete.

First, I sipped the clear, sweetish water in the center. Then the vendor showed me how to use a shard of shell to scoop out the soft, white custardy jelly—the part that, if aged, would one day become the crisp meat inside a hard-shelled coconut. Green coconuts are harvested at six months of age and can be purchased at Hispanic and Caribbean markets. It takes about a year for the flesh to ripen and harden to the point where it can be munched or grated. The ripe (brown) coconuts sold at supermarkets have been stripped of the husks.

Choosing and storing When buying ripe coconuts, avoid those with wet eyes (the markings on the stem end), cracked shells, or a sour or acrid aroma. The coconut should feel heavy in your hand, and you should be able to hear the coconut water slosh around when you shake it. Store whole coconuts at room temperature for a couple of weeks.

Getting to the meat To get to the meat, you must first drain the coconut and then crack it open. To drain a coconut, punch out the "eyes" using a screwdriver (preferably a Phillips-head) and hammer. Invert the coconut over a measuring cup and shake out the liquid. Save it for drinking—it has a slightly sweet taste with a light coconut scent. Although commonly called coconut milk, this is actually coconut water. Next, wrap the coconut in a clean dish towel and whack it with a hammer. It should break into five or six pieces.

Bake the pieces on a baking sheet at 400°F for 10 to 15 minutes or until the meat begins to pull away from the shell. Using a table knife, pry the meat away from the shell and cut off the brown skin.

The meat is now ready for munching, grating, shredding or shaving into thin strips. To shred or grate coconut, use a food processor. To cut coconut shavings, use a mandoline or thin slicing blade in a food processor.

One coconut yields ½ to 1 cup water and 3 to 3½ cups grated flesh. Three cups grated flesh makes an equal amount of milk.

Coconut Beef Saté with Peanut Sauce

double thickness. Place foil on half of grill. Place satés on gas grill over medium heat or on charcoal grill 4 to 6 inches from medium coals; skewer handles should be over foil to prevent burning. Cook 2 to 3 minutes or until no longer pink, turning once. Serve immediately with Peanut Sauce.

24 satés.

PER SATE: 120 calories, 9.5 g total fat (5 g saturated fat), 5 g protein, 4 g carbohydrate, 10 mg cholesterol, 165 mg sodium, 1.5 g fiber.

Peanut Sauce

Peanut sauce is the requisite accompaniment to saté in most of Southeast Asia, where its sweet nutty flavor goes perfectly with smoky charred chicken, pork or beef. Here's a quick version that can be made in a food processor in a couple of minutes.

1   medium tomato, peeled, seeded, diced
1   jalapeño chile, minced (leave seeds in for a hotter version)
⅓   cup chopped fresh cilantro
¾   cup chunky peanut butter
½   cup unsweetened coconut milk
1   tablespoon fish sauce or soy sauce
2   teaspoons lime juice

Place tomato, chile and cilantro in food processor; process until finely ground. Add all remaining ingredients; process until blended.

Coconut-Pineapple Rice

The coconut and pineapple give this pilaf a Polynesian accent. The recipe calls for fresh coconut, but in a pinch you could use packaged shredded coconut.

2   tablespoons butter
1   small onion, finely chopped
2   teaspoons finely chopped fresh ginger
1   garlic clove, minced
½   cup shredded fresh coconut
1½ cups converted long-grain rice
¾   cup coconut milk
¾   cup reduced-sodium chicken broth or vegetable broth
1   cup cubed pineapple (½ inch)
1   teaspoon salt
⅛   teaspoon white pepper
2   tablespoons chopped fresh cilantro

1 Heat oven to 350°F. Melt butter in large ovenproof skillet. Add onion, ginger and garlic; cook over medium heat 3 minutes or until soft but not brown. Add coconut; cook 30 seconds. Add rice; cook 30 seconds or until grains are shiny.

2 Stir in coconut milk, broth, pineapple, salt and pepper. Bring to a boil. (Do not stir.) Cover.

3 Bake 15 to 20 minutes or until rice is tender and liquid is absorbed. Check rice after 15 minutes; if rice is tender but moist, remove cover and continue baking 5 to 8 minutes. Fluff rice with fork; sprinkle with cilantro.

9 (½-cup) servings.

PER SERVING: 235 calories, 8 g total fat (6 g saturated fat), 4.5 g protein, 36.5 g carbohydrate, 5 mg cholesterol, 330 mg sodium, 1.5 g fiber.

Coconut Chips

Rich, sweet and audibly crisp, these handsome toasted coconut chips are a popular snack in Barbados. They're simply seasoned here so you can appreciate the taste of the coconut. You could certainly spice up the seasoning with cumin, coriander or cayenne pepper.

  1 coconut
  ¼ teaspoon salt

1 Crack open and shell coconut. Peel away brown skin. With knife, vegetable peeler or food processor fitted with slicing blade, cut coconut pieces into thin (⅟₁₆-inch) strips. Heat oven to 300°F.

2 Arrange coconut strips on baking sheet. Bake 40 to 60 minutes or until lightly browned and crisp, turning chips occasionally to ensure even browning. Sprinkle with salt. Store in airtight container.

3 cups.

PER ½ CUP: 235 calories, 22 g total fat (19.5 g saturated fat), 2 g protein, 10 g carbohydrate, 0 mg cholesterol, 110 mg sodium, 6 g fiber.

Coconut Milk

For much of the world, coconut meat is not an end in itself, but a source of coconut milk. The fat in coconut milk makes it a rich ingredient, which is used in several recipes here.

To make coconut milk, shredded fresh coconut is mixed with boiling water, then strained through cheesecloth. To make thick coconut milk, use equal parts grated coconut and water. Thin coconut milk is made by repeating the process with the coconut used for making an earlier batch of milk.

Making coconut milk isn't difficult, but canned coconut milk can be substituted. Be sure to buy coconut milk without sugar. You can find it in the Asian section of grocery stores or in Asian, Caribbean or Brazilian grocery stores. One of the best brands is Chaokoh from Thailand.

Coconut milk is often confused with coconut cream. The latter is a sugary product made in Puerto Rico and elsewhere in the Caribbean. It's an essential ingredient in a piña colada and other tropical drinks. The best known brand is Coco López.

Basic Coconut Milk
  3 cups freshly grated coconut
      (from 1 coconut)
  3 cups boiling water

1 Place coconut and water in blender or food processor; blend until well combined. (Use caution when blending hot liquid.) Pour into large bowl. Let stand at room temperature 30 to 60 minutes to allow flavors to blend.

2 Strain mixture through several layers of cheesecloth, twisting tightly to extract milk. (If desired, use the same coconut flesh to make a thin coconut milk by repeating the process above.) (Coconut milk can be refrigerated up to 5 days or frozen up to 3 months.)

3 cups.

PER CUP: 85 calories, 9 g total fat (8 g saturated fat), 1 g protein, 4 g carbohydrate, 0 mg cholesterol, 5 mg sodium, 0 g fiber.

Coconut Crack-Up

To break a coconut into equal halves for the Coco Loco Brûlée, tap the shell with the claw side of a hammer along an imaginary line going around the middle. After 10 to 20 taps, the shell should break in two. Work over a towel.

Peaches and
Pork

Peach and Bourbon-Glazed Pork
with Peach and Pecan Chutney

A buffet dinner showcases the new direction of Southern cooking.

Text and Recipes by Ray Overton

Ask native Southerners what makes them proud and chances are they'll say it's their Southern heritage and hospitality, coupled with their ability to adapt to change. It's this ability that has placed the South in the midst of a culinary revolution. The fried foods, heavy gravies and slow-simmered vegetables that once prevailed have been gently nudged aside. In their places are creative dishes that blend the best of the old with the innovations of the new—indigenous ingredients with a global influence.

This contemporary definition of Southern cooking is reflected in this entertaining menu for a buffet dinner. The main dish features Southern favorites —pork, bourbon, pecans and peaches—with updated twists of a smoky-sweet glaze and a curried chutney. A side dish of peas and potatoes, Southern staples, is topped with a tangy dressing and served chilled. Dessert is a poppy seed cake flecked with citrus. It's topped with a modern version of an old favorite—seven-minute frosting.

Welcome your friends and family with a touch of old-fashioned Southern hospitality and a healthy serving of new Southern cooking.

Peach and Bourbon-Glazed Pork with Peach and Pecan Chutney

The ports of Charleston and Savannah were central to the expansion of the developing South. The spice trade and the tradition of pairing homegrown products with more exotic ingredients carry over into today's way of cooking. Here, a delicious pork, glazed with sweet peaches and smoky bourbon, is accompanied by a discreet curried peach and pecan chutney.

GLAZE
- ½ cup peach preserves
- ¼ cup bourbon whiskey or peach nectar
- ¼ cup fresh orange juice
- 1 tablespoon chopped fresh ginger
- 1 tablespoon chopped fresh rosemary
- 1¾ teaspoons grated orange peel
- ¼ teaspoon crushed red pepper
- 2 garlic cloves, chopped

PORK
- 1 (4-lb.) boneless pork loin
- ½ teaspoon salt
- ¼ teaspoon freshly ground black pepper

CHUTNEY
- 2 tablespoons olive oil
- 1 medium onion, chopped
- 1 tablespoon curry powder
- 2 medium garlic cloves, minced
- 1 (16-oz.) pkg. frozen sliced peaches, thawed, or 4 to 5 fresh peaches, peeled, pitted, sliced
- ⅔ cup packed brown sugar
- ½ cup golden raisins

½ cup apple cider vinegar
½ cup apple juice
2 tablespoons chopped fresh ginger
1 teaspoon chopped fresh rosemary
½ teaspoon salt
¼ teaspoon freshly ground black pepper
½ cup chopped pecans, lightly toasted

1 Heat oven to 400°F. In medium bowl, combine all glaze ingredients.

2 Spray large shallow roasting pan with nonstick cooking spray. Sprinkle pork loin with ½ teaspoon salt and ¼ teaspoon pepper. Place in pan. (Cut pork in half if too long for pan.) Brush with glaze. Add ½ cup water to pan.

3 Bake 45 to 50 minutes or until internal temperature reaches 150°F, brushing with glaze every 10 minutes. Let pork stand loosely covered 15 minutes before slicing.

4 Meanwhile, heat oil in large skillet over medium heat until hot. Add onion; cook 3 minutes. Add curry powder and garlic; cook 2 minutes or until onion is tender. Stir in all remaining ingredients except pecans. Reduce heat to low; simmer, uncovered, 25 to 30 minutes or until mixture is very thick, stirring occasionally. Stir in pecans. (Chutney can be made up to 1 week ahead. Cover and refrigerate.) Serve at room temperature with pork.

12 servings.

PER SERVING: 385 calories, 11.5 g total fat (2.5 g saturated fat), 35 g protein, 33 g carbohydrate, 95 mg cholesterol, 280 mg sodium, 2 g fiber.

Black-Eyed Pea and Rice Salad

This very versatile Southern side dish is perfect as a chilled salad, a bed for grilled pork chops or chicken breasts, or as an appetizer served with tortilla chips or toasted pita wedges. For optimal taste, make it a day ahead to allow the flavors to mingle.

3 cups frozen black-eyed peas
¾ cup long-grain rice

2 slices thick-cut bacon, coarsely chopped
½ large Vidalia onion, chopped
2 medium garlic cloves, chopped
⅓ cup apple cider vinegar
1 tablespoon sugar
⅓ cup chopped pimientos, drained
½ cucumber, seeded, finely chopped
½ green bell pepper, chopped
1 or 2 jalapeño chiles, seeded, finely chopped
¼ cup chopped fresh cilantro
1½ teaspoons salt
1½ teaspoons ground cumin
¼ teaspoon freshly ground pepper
2 tablespoons fresh lime juice

1 In large pot or Dutch oven, cook black-eyed peas and rice in boiling salted water 20 to 25 minutes or until tender. Drain; rinse with cold running water. Drain well; place in large bowl.

2 Cook bacon in large skillet over medium-high heat 8 to 10 minutes or until crisp. Remove bacon from skillet; drain on paper towels.

3 Add onion to bacon drippings in skillet; cook over medium heat 6 to 8 minutes or until tender. Add garlic; cook an additional 1 minute. Stir in vinegar and sugar. Cook 3 minutes or until liquid is reduced by half.

4 Add onion mixture to black-eyed peas and rice. Stir in all remaining ingredients except bacon. Cover; refrigerate at least 4 hours or overnight.

5 Just before serving, top with bacon. Serve chilled or at room temperature.

12 (½-cup) servings.

PER SERVING: 105 calories, 1.5 g total fat (.5 g saturated fat), 3 g protein, 20.5 g carbohydrate, 0 mg cholesterol, 540 mg sodium, 2.5 g fiber.

Vine-Ripened Tomato and Corn Platter

For all its simplicity, this salad is a winner every time. Try to find the ripest tomatoes around, preferably from a farmers' market or roadside produce stand.

4 ears corn
8 large tomatoes, sliced (¼ inch)
1 small Vidalia onion, halved, thinly sliced
4 green onions, chopped
3 tablespoons extra-virgin olive oil
3 tablespoons balsamic vinegar
1 teaspoon salt
½ teaspoon freshly ground pepper
¾ cup (3 oz.) crumbled feta cheese
¼ cup chopped fresh basil

1 Cook corn in large saucepan of boiling salted water 3 minutes. Place in bowl of ice water to stop cooking. When cool, drain and pat dry. With knife, cut kernels from cobs.

2 Arrange tomato slices on large platter. Top with corn, Vidalia onion and green onions. (Salad can be made to this point up to 3 hours ahead. Cover and refrigerate. Serve at room temperature.)

3 Drizzle salad with oil and vinegar. Sprinkle with salt, pepper, cheese and basil.

12 servings.

PER SERVING: 115 calories, 5.5 g total fat (1.5 g saturated fat), 3.5 g protein, 15.5 g carbohydrate, 5 mg cholesterol, 295 mg sodium, 2.5 g fiber.

Minted Sugar Snap Peas and Potatoes with Raspberry-Mint Dressing

VEGETABLES
1 lb. fresh sugar snap peas
1 lb. tiny new red potatoes, quartered
1½ teaspoons vegetable oil
1½ teaspoons finely chopped fresh ginger
1½ medium garlic cloves, chopped
½ red onion, halved, thinly sliced
½ red bell pepper, cut into ¼-inch strips
½ yellow bell pepper, cut into ¼-inch strips
⅓ cup lightly salted shelled sunflower seeds

DRESSING
¼ cup raspberry vinegar
1 tablespoon coarse Dijon mustard
½ teaspoon sugar
½ teaspoon salt

⅛ teaspoon freshly ground
   black pepper
2 tablespoons extra-virgin
   olive oil
4 tablespoons chopped
   fresh mint

1 Cook sugar snap peas in large saucepan of boiling salted water 3 minutes or until crisp-tender. Remove peas with large strainer; rinse with cold running water. Drain well; place in large bowl.

2 Add potatoes to same boiling water; cook 10 to 12 minutes or just until tender. Drain; rinse with cold running water. Drain well; add to sugar snap peas.

3 Heat vegetable oil in large skillet over medium-high heat until hot. Add ginger and garlic; cook

30 seconds. Add onion, red bell pepper and yellow bell pepper; cook 2 minutes or until crisp-tender. Place in bowl with sugar snap peas.

4 In small bowl, whisk together vinegar, mustard, sugar, salt and pepper. Slowly whisk in olive oil. Stir in 2 tablespoons of the mint. Drizzle dressing over vegetables; toss to coat. Cover; refrigerate at least 2 hours.

5 To serve, place vegetables on large platter. Top with remaining 2 tablespoons mint and sunflower seeds. Serve chilled or at room temperature.

12 (about ⅔-cup) servings.

PER SERVING: 100 calories, 5 g total fat (.5 g saturated fat), 3 g protein, 12.5 g carbohydrate, 0 mg cholesterol, 165 mg sodium, 2.5 g fiber.

Vanilla-Poppy Seed Layer Cake with Sunshine Frosting

This stunning creation easily appeases the notorious Southern sweet tooth. The moist vanilla cake is enhanced with orange juice, sweet sherry and the unmistakable crunch of tiny poppy seeds. The fluffy frosting, with its delicate specks of orange peel, is an updated rendition of the classic seven-minute frosting.

CAKE
½ cup unsalted butter, softened
1¼ cups sugar
3 eggs, separated
3 cups cake flour
1 tablespoon baking powder
½ teaspoon salt
1⅓ cups milk
1 tablespoon vanilla
½ cup poppy seeds
½ cup fresh orange juice
¼ cup cream sherry, if desired

FROSTING
2 egg whites
½ cup sugar
2 tablespoons water
⅛ teaspoon salt
1 (7-oz.) jar marshmallow creme
¼ teaspoon orange extract
1½ teaspoons grated orange peel

1 Heat oven to 350°F. Lightly spray 2 (9x2-inch) round cake pans with nonstick cooking spray. Line bottoms of pans with parchment paper; spray paper. Lightly flour pans and paper.

2 In large bowl, beat butter and 1 cup of the sugar at medium speed 5 minutes or until light and fluffy. Add egg yolks one at a time, beating 20 seconds after each addition.

3 On waxed paper, sift together flour, baking powder and ½ teaspoon salt. At low speed, add to sugar mixture alternately with milk, beginning and ending with dry ingredients. Beat in 1 tablespoon vanilla and poppy seeds.

4 In another large bowl, beat 3 egg whites at medium-high speed until soft peaks form. Gradually add remaining ¼ cup sugar 1 tablespoon at a time, beating until whites are

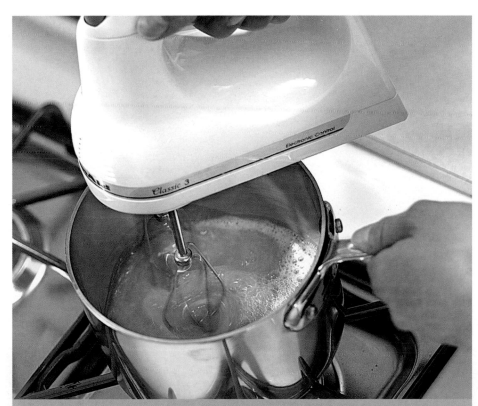

Cooking the Frosting

The frosting for Vanilla-Poppy Seed Layer Cake is a variation on seven-minute frosting. The traditional seven-minute frosting is usually cooked in a bowl over a pan of water. In contrast, our version is cooked directly over the heat. Beat the mixture constantly, so that the egg whites don't overcook, until the mixture reaches 160°F.

very glossy and stiff. Stir ⅓ of egg whites into batter to lighten. Fold in remaining egg whites. Spread batter evenly in pans.

5 Bake 25 to 30 minutes or until toothpick inserted in center comes out clean. Cool on wire rack 5 minutes. Remove from pans.

6 In small bowl, combine orange juice and sherry. With toothpick, pierce cake layers several times. Brush warm cake layers with orange juice mixture. (It seems like a lot, but the cake will absorb all the liquid.) Cool completely.

7 In large heavy saucepan, combine 2 egg whites, ½ cup sugar, water and ⅛ teaspoon salt. Cook over medium heat, beating constantly at low speed, 4 to 6 minutes or until temperature reaches 160°F. Remove from heat; beat at medium-high speed 3 to 4 minutes or until soft peaks form. Add marshmallow creme. Continue beating 3 to 5 minutes or until stiff peaks begin to form. Stir in orange extract and orange peel.

8 To assemble, place 1 cake layer on serving plate. Spread with 1 cup frosting. Top with second cake layer. Spread sides and top of cake with remaining frosting. Refrigerate until ready to serve. Store in refrigerator.

12 servings.

PER SERVING: 405 calories, 12 g total fat (6 g saturated fat), 6.5 g protein, 68.5 g carbohydrate, 75 mg cholesterol, 290 mg sodium, 1.5 g fiber.

Vanilla-Poppy Seed Layer Cake with Sunshine Frosting

Honey-Cardamom Cake with Orange Blossom Cream

From light and fruity to tangy and rich, your honey choices have never been greater.

Text and Recipes by Gene Opton

Not so long ago, when a recipe called for honey, you didn't have to give much thought as to which kind to use. With so few options, and many honeys labeled as wildflower—or simply "honey"—it didn't really matter.

Today you have many more choices. Some producers who once blended various honeys are now keeping them separate and labeling them according to the source of the nectar. Blueberry, sunflower, buckwheat and tupelo are just a sampling of single-flower honeys being sold today. Your options also have increased because the honey sold locally is no longer limited to what is produced locally.

Unlike sugar, which is a neutral sweetener, honey has distinctive flavors, ranging from mild to strong. Now with the abundance of varieties, your choices for creating flavor nuances in honey-sweetened recipes are greater than ever. So bring home some honey, get out a spoon and discover your personal favorites. Then get cooking!

Honey-Cardamom Cake with Orange Blossom Cream

Honey lends its distinctive flavor to this delicately spiced, wonderfully moist cake. It's lovely with just a dollop of honeyed whipped cream, or serve it with sliced peaches or nectarines. Use orange blossom honey or another mild honey, such as clover.

CAKE
- 3 cups cake flour
- 1 tablespoon baking powder
- 2 teaspoons ground cardamom
- ½ teaspoon salt
- ¾ cup mild honey
- ½ cup unsalted butter, softened
- ¾ cup sugar
- 3 eggs
- 1 cup whole milk

SYRUP
- ¼ cup honey
- ¼ cup hot water

CREAM
- 2 cups whipping cream
- ¼ cup orange blossom honey

1 Heat oven to 325°F. Spray 13x9-inch pan with nonstick cooking spray. In medium bowl, stir together flour, baking powder, cardamom and ½ teaspoon salt.

2 In large bowl, beat ¾ cup honey and butter at medium speed 2 minutes. Slowly add sugar, beating constantly. Add eggs one at a time, beating 1 minute after each addition. Add dry ingredients alternately with milk, beginning and ending with dry ingredients. Spread evenly in pan.

Grilled Chicken with Honey and Rosemary

3 Bake 40 to 45 minutes or until toothpick inserted in center comes out clean. Cool in pan on wire rack 10 minutes.

4 Meanwhile, stir together syrup ingredients.

5 With long wooden skewer, poke holes in cake, poking through to bottom of pan. Brush cake with syrup. Cool completely.

6 In medium bowl, beat cream at medium-high speed until soft peaks form. Add ¼ cup honey, beating just until blended. Serve cake with cream. Store in refrigerator.

12 servings.

PER SERVING: 475 calories, 22 g total fat (13.5 g saturated fat), 6 g protein, 65 g carbohydrate, 120 mg cholesterol, 285 mg sodium, .5 g fiber.

Grilled Chicken with Honey and Rosemary

Summer calls for quick recipes, and this one couldn't be easier. The three-ingredient marinade/glaze marries sweet honey and assertive rosemary, with tasty results.

    6 tablespoons honey
    1 tablespoon chopped fresh
         rosemary or 1 teaspoon dried
 1½ teaspoons Worcestershire sauce
    4 boneless skinless chicken
         breast halves
    ¼ teaspoon salt
    ⅛ teaspoon freshly ground pepper

1 In small bowl, blend honey, rosemary and Worcestershire sauce. Reserve 3 tablespoons to brush on chicken during grilling. Place chicken in glass baking dish; pour remaining honey mixture over chicken. Let stand at room temperature 30 minutes to marinate, or cover and refrigerate overnight.

2 Heat grill. Remove chicken from marinade; discard marinade. Sprinkle with salt and pepper. Place chicken on gas grill over medium heat or on charcoal grill 4 to 6 inches from medium coals. Cook 6 to 8 minutes or until juices run clear, turning once and brushing with reserved marinade.

Sweet Choices

Dozens of varieties of honey are produced in the United States. Some, like creamed honey, are best used as spreads on bread, while others make delightful substitutes for sugar in cooking. If you can't find a particular variety in your local store, check the National Honey Board's Web site for information on suppliers: www.nhb.org.

Forms Peruse the honey section in a large supermarket, and you're likely to find honey in a variety of styles.

♦ Liquid honey is extracted from the comb, filtered and packed into jars.

♦ Creamed or spun honey is honey that has been spun to create a thick, creamy texture that is ideal for spreading.

♦ Comb honey is packaged in the comb, just as it comes from the hive. Squares of larger comb are cut and fitted into boxes. The beeswax of the honeycomb is completely edible, and comb honey can be eaten like chewy candy. Sometimes you'll find a jar of liquid honey to which a piece of cut comb has been added.

Flavors The specific flavor of each honey depends on the particular nectar the bees gather. When bees collect nectar from large growths of one certain blossom, the honey is labeled "single-flower" honey; examples are clover, lavender, sunflower and star thistle. Sometimes bees gather nectar from a variety of sources, making multi-floral honey called "wildflower." Flavors range from light and fruity to tangy and rich.

As a general rule, light-colored honey is mild in flavor, while dark honey is more assertive. Clover, acacia, basswood and orange blossom are some of the lighter varieties; they make wonderful sweeteners for cereal, tea, fruit salads and salad dressings. In the middle range, you find star thistle, Florida tupelo, sage, alfalfa and honeys from berry blossoms, which add a stronger flavor. Dark honey, such as buckwheat, is used like brown sugar or molasses; it works well on oatmeal, and in pancakes and whole-grain breads.

Flavored honeys are those to which flavoring agents, such as fruit or herb essences, have been added.

Taste Doing a honey taste test will help you discover the distinctive flavor differences between varieties, and you can choose the one that pleases you most. It only takes a few minutes. When you open the jar, notice the aroma of the honey, which is strongest at this point. Spoon out a small amount of the honey, less than ⅛ teaspoon, and taste it slowly, noticing how the flavor spreads in your mouth. Notice, too, the aftertaste, which is an important component in the flavor of honey. If you are comparing several different kinds of honey—one each of the light, medium and dark varieties makes an interesting combination—give your palate a short rest between tastes. Dairy products help you taste the nuances of a particular honey; try honey drizzled on plain yogurt.

Cooking Hints

♦ Use liquid honey, not creamed or comb, in cooking.

♦ Honey tastes sweeter than sugar. When substituting honey for sugar (other than in baked goods), start by using half as much honey as sugar; then adjust to taste. Choose a mild honey when you want to sweeten a dish without making a major flavor change.

♦ In baking, honey changes the texture of breads and cakes, and it keeps them from going stale. To substitute honey for sugar in baked goods, begin by replacing half the sugar called for with honey. For example, if a cake recipe calls for 2 cups of sugar, use 1 cup sugar and substitute ½ cup honey for the other 1 cup sugar. For every cup of honey used, reduce the liquid in the recipe ¼ cup and add ½ teaspoon baking soda. Because honey causes baked goods to brown faster than sugar, you need to reduce the oven temperature called for in the original recipe by 25°F.

♦ Almost all honey crystallizes; it's a natural change and does not mean the honey has spoiled. Some packagers strain and heat the honey to slow the crystallization process, but doing so can reduce the aroma and flavor of the honey. To reliquefy crystallized honey, place it in a container of warm water and allow it to stand several hours or overnight. Repeat as necessary.

---

4 servings.

PER SERVING: 200 calories, 4 g total fat (1 g saturated fat), 26.5 g protein, 13.5 g carbohydrate, 75 mg cholesterol, 225 mg sodium, 0 g fiber.

Roasted Beets in Honey Sauce

You have the option of serving this side dish cold or hot. Cold, the beets are more tangy and relish-like. When served hot, the flavor mellows a bit with the addition of butter. Either way, it's delicious!

1½ lbs. small beets*
3 tablespoons cider vinegar
3 tablespoons mild honey
⅛ teaspoon salt
⅛ teaspoon freshly ground pepper
¼ teaspoon grated orange peel

1 Heat oven to 425°F. Line rimmed baking sheet with foil. Cut tops off beets, leaving 1 inch of stem. Place in single layer in pan; cover tightly with foil. Bake 1 hour or until fork-tender. Cool until still warm but easy to handle. Peel beets while warm; cut into ½-inch pieces.

2 In medium bowl, stir together all remaining ingredients except orange peel. Stir in beets; sprinkle with orange peel.** (Dish can be made up to 1 week ahead. Cover and refrigerate.)

TIPS *One 15-oz. can baby beets, drained, can be substituted for the roasted beets. Omit the roasting step.

**To serve beets warm, heat sauce and add 1 tablespoon butter. Stir in beets; heat until warm.

6 servings.

PER SERVING: 80 calories, 0 g total fat (0 g saturated fat), 2 g protein, 20 g carbohydrate, 0 mg cholesterol, 135 mg sodium, 2 g fiber.

Chewy Honey Bars

This very low-tech recipe fits right into summer schedules, when you want to spend plenty of time outdoors. You use only a saucepan, bowl, spoon and pan to make chewy bar cookies that travel and keep well.

1 cup all-purpose flour
1 teaspoon baking soda
1 teaspoon ground ginger
½ teaspoon salt
½ teaspoon cinnamon
   Dash cloves
¼ cup unsalted butter
¾ cup mild or dark honey
1 egg
1 teaspoon vanilla
1 cup chopped walnuts

1 Heat oven to 325°F. Spray 9-inch square pan with nonstick cooking spray. In small bowl, stir together flour, baking soda, ginger, salt, cinnamon and cloves.

2 Melt butter in medium saucepan over low heat. Remove from heat. Stir in honey until well blended. Let stand until saucepan is just warm to the touch.

3 Whisk egg into honey mixture. Stir in vanilla and flour mixture. Batter should be smooth and thin. Stir in walnuts. Pour into pan.

4 Bake 20 to 25 minutes or until toothpick inserted in center comes out almost clean, with a few crumbs remaining. Cool in pan. (Bars will sink slightly as they cool.) Store in airtight container.

16 bars.

PER BAR: 160 calories, 8 g total fat (2.5 g saturated fat), 2.5 g protein, 21.5 g carbohydrate, 20 mg cholesterol, 160 mg sodium, .5 g fiber.

Honey Cheesecake with Blueberry Sauce

Creamy cheese is a particularly effective carrier for honey flavors. Use a light, luscious fruit honey, such as alfalfa, blueberry or blackberry, and notice the subtly different results.

CRUST
1½ cups graham cracker crumbs
5 tablespoons unsalted butter, melted
2 tablespoons sugar

Romaine Salad with Honey-Lime Vinaigrette

FILLING

- 1 (8-oz.) pkg. cream cheese, cut up, softened
- 1 (15-oz.) container whole-milk ricotta cheese
- ½ cup honey
- ½ teaspoon salt
- ¾ cup half-and-half
- 3 eggs
- 2 tablespoons all-purpose flour

SAUCE

- 4 cups blueberries
- ½ cup honey
- 2 tablespoons fresh lemon juice

1 Heat oven to 400°F. In medium bowl, stir together all crust ingredients. Press in bottom and 1 inch up sides of 9-inch springform pan. Bake 5 to 8 minutes or until very lightly browned. Cool completely.

2 Reduce oven temperature to 325°F. Place cream cheese and ricotta in food processor; process 20 to 30 seconds or until very smooth. Add ½ cup honey and salt; process briefly to blend. Add half-and-half and eggs; process until smooth. Sprinkle flour over mixture; process briefly to combine. Pour into crust-lined pan.

3 Bake at 325°F for 60 to 65 minutes or until top looks dull and is dry to the touch. Center should move slightly when side of pan is tapped but should not ripple as if liquid. Cool cheesecake on wire rack, away from drafts, 2 to 3 hours or until completely cooled. Cover; refrigerate at least 4 hours or overnight.

4 Place 2 cups of the blueberries and ½ cup honey in small saucepan. Cook over medium heat 10 minutes or until soft and thickened, stirring occasionally. Press mixture through strainer into small bowl containing remaining 2 cups berries. Gently stir in lemon juice. Serve over cheesecake. Store in refrigerator.

12 servings.

PER SERVING: 375 calories, 20 g total fat (12 g saturated fat), 8.5 g protein, 43.5 g carbohydrate, 110 mg cholesterol, 270 mg sodium, 1 g fiber.

Romaine Salad with Honey-Lime Vinaigrette

If you can get baby romaine in your local market, its crisp leaves lend the perfect crunch to this brightly flavored salad. Honey balances the tangy acid of fresh lime juice in the dressing, which can be mixed a day or two ahead.

DRESSING

- 4 teaspoons fresh lime juice
- 2 teaspoons mild honey
- ¼ teaspoon salt
  Dash cayenne pepper
- 3 tablespoons vegetable oil

SALAD

- 4 cups chopped romaine lettuce
- ½ cup halved strawberries
- 1 avocado, cut into ½-inch pieces

1 In small bowl, whisk together lime juice, honey, salt and cayenne pepper. Add oil; whisk until thoroughly blended. (Dressing can be made up to 2 days ahead. Cover and refrigerate. Whisk to blend before using.)

2 In large bowl, combine lettuce, strawberries, avocado and dressing; toss to coat evenly.

4 servings.

PER SERVING: 185 calories, 17 g total fat (2.5 g saturated fat), 2 g protein, 9 g carbohydrate, 0 mg cholesterol, 160 mg sodium, 3.5 g fiber.

All-American
Grill

Grilled Strip Steaks with Multi-Mustard Sauce

There's a good reason for centering a meal on steak! It tastes good, cooks quickly and needs little enhancement.

Text and Recipes by Melanie Barnard

It's been five decades since grilling became a hot-ticket item for backyard entertaining. Back in the '50s, chicken, burgers, hot dogs and potatoes wrapped in foil were barbecue staples, cooked on wobbly metal braziers.

Today, whole cookbooks are devoted to grilling, and barbecue equipment has become far more sophisticated. But one thing hasn't changed: Special occasions still call for steak.

There's good reason for centering a meal on steak: Not only does it taste good, it cooks quickly and needs little enhancement. And it's easy to build a menu around steak. A favorite accompaniment is potatoes, but why not try sweet potatoes brushed with a molasses glaze? Add a spinach salad with summer tomatoes and America's own Maytag blue cheese. Round out the menu with a twist on a classic—shortcake in the form of a tart.

Grilled Strip Steaks with Multi-Mustard Sauce

Grilling imparts a mellow flavor to the mustard sauce that's slathered onto the meat, giving complexity to the dish without extra work. This treatment is also terrific on chicken or pork chops.

- ½ cup Dijon mustard
- 4 tablespoons chopped fresh tarragon
- 4 tablespoons cognac, brandy or apple juice
- 3 tablespoons olive oil
- 3 tablespoons white wine vinegar
- 1½ teaspoons dry mustard
- 1½ teaspoons mustard seeds
- 1½ teaspoons multi-peppercorn blend
- 1½ teaspoons cracked or freshly ground pepper
- 6 (6-oz.) beef top loin steaks (1 inch thick)*

1 In small bowl, stir together Dijon mustard, 2 tablespoons of the tarragon, 2 tablespoons of the cognac, oil, vinegar, dry mustard, mustard seeds, peppercorn blend and pepper. Reserve ¼ cup sauce for grilling. Into remaining sauce, stir in remaining 2 tablespoons tarragon and 2 tablespoons cognac; reserve for steak topping.

2 Heat grill. Brush grilling sauce generously on both sides of each steak. Let stand 15 to 20 minutes at room temperature or refrigerate up to 4 hours before cooking.

3 Place steaks on gas grill over medium-high heat or on charcoal grill 4 to 6 inches from medium-high coals. Cook 6 to 8 minutes for

Strawberry-Blueberry Shortcake Tart

medium-rare or until of desired doneness, turning once. Remove steaks from grill. Spoon reserved sauce over steaks; let stand 2 to 3 minutes.

TIP *Loin steaks are also called New York, Kansas City or strip steaks.

6 servings.

PER SERVING: 525 calories, 27.5 g total fat (8 g saturated fat), 56.5 g protein, 4.5 g carbohydrate, 145 mg cholesterol, 690 mg sodium, .5 g fiber.

Strawberry-Blueberry Shortcake Tart

The all-American strawberry short-cake was the inspiration for this scrumptious dessert. Blueberries make a wonderful partner for strawberries, but you could substitute any summer fruit (except watermelon)—just be sure the total fruit is about 5 cups.

CRUST

1   cup all-purpose flour
2   tablespoons sugar
1   teaspoon baking powder
¼   teaspoon baking soda
¼   teaspoon salt
¼   cup butter, chilled, cut up
⅓   cup sour cream
1   egg white
¼   cup sliced almonds

FILLING
- ½ cup sugar
- 2 tablespoons cornstarch
- ¾ cup orange juice
- ¼ cup Grand Marnier, other orange-flavored liqueur or additional orange juice
- 4 cups small strawberries or sliced larger berries
- 1 cup blueberries

ALMOND CREAM
- 1 cup heavy whipping cream
- ¼ cup powdered sugar
- ¼ cup sour cream
- ¼ teaspoon almond extract

1 Heat oven to 425°F. Spray 9-inch pie plate with nonstick cooking spray. In food processor, combine flour, 2 tablespoons sugar, baking powder, baking soda and salt; pulse to mix. Add butter evenly over flour; process a few seconds until mixture resembles coarse crumbs with some pea-size pieces. Add ⅓ cup sour cream; pulse just until clumps begin to form. (If dough seems dry, add water 1 teaspoon at a time.)

2 Press dough into ball; knead dough a few seconds until smooth. Press evenly in bottom and up sides of pie plate. Beat egg white until frothy; brush over pastry. Sprinkle with almonds. Bake 12 to 15 minutes or until golden brown. Cool completely on wire rack.

3 In small saucepan, whisk together ½ cup sugar and cornstarch. Whisk in orange juice and liqueur. Cook over medium heat until mixture comes to a full boil, thickens and becomes glossy, whisking constantly.

4 Place strawberries and blueberries in medium bowl. Pour hot sauce over berries; stir to mix thoroughly. Cool about 10 minutes.

5 Pour berry mixture evenly into baked crust. Refrigerate at least 1 hour or up to 8 hours, until set and berries are chilled.

6 Right before serving, in medium bowl, beat all almond cream ingredients until soft peaks form. Serve over tart. Store in refrigerator.

8 servings.

PER SERVING: 410 calories, 22 g total fat (12.5 g saturated fat), 4.5 g protein, 47.5 g carbohydrate, 65 mg cholesterol, 205 mg sodium, 3 g fiber.

Molasses-Blackened Sweet Potato Slices

The heat of the grill caramelizes the natural sugars in both the molasses and sweet potatoes, resulting in blackened edges and a pleasant charred taste. Buy large sweet potatoes so that the lengthwise slices will be bigger and easier to manage on the grill.

- ¼ cup vegetable oil
- 2 tablespoons molasses
- 2 teaspoons lemon juice
- ½ teaspoon salt
- ½ teaspoon freshly ground pepper
- ¼ teaspoon hot pepper sauce
- 1½ lbs. sweet potatoes* (about 3 medium), peeled, cut lengthwise into ¼-inch slices

1 Heat grill. In small dish, stir together all ingredients except sweet potatoes. Place sweet potato slices on tray; brush both sides of each slice with molasses mixture.

2 Place sweet potatoes on gas grill over medium heat or on charcoal grill 4 to 6 inches from medium coals. Cook 10 to 12 minutes or until grill marks form, edges are lightly charred and sweet potatoes are tender, turning once and brushing with any remaining molasses mixture. (If grilling sweet potatoes before meat, push finished slices to side of grill, or place on sheet of foil and move to edge of grill to keep warm.)

TIP *Look for the deep orange-colored sweet potatoes, often labeled as yams.

6 servings.

PER SERVING: 190 calories, 9 g total fat (1.5 g saturated fat), 1.5 g protein, 26.5 g carbohydrate, 0 mg cholesterol, 210 mg sodium, 2.5 g fiber.

Tomato and Maytag Blue Salad

Alternating slices of red and yellow tomatoes with the onion is attractive, but it is far more important to use ripe, garden-fresh, meaty tomatoes than to worry about perfect color. Likewise, greens should reflect what's best and freshest from the farm stand or your garden.

VINAIGRETTE
- ⅓ cup olive oil
- ¼ cup balsamic vinegar
- 3 garlic cloves, minced
- ½ teaspoon salt
- ½ teaspoon freshly ground pepper

SALAD
- 1 (10-oz.) pkg. spinach leaves (8 cups)
- ½ cup fresh basil
- 3 medium red and/or yellow tomatoes, sliced
- 1 small Vidalia onion, sliced
- 1 cup (4 oz.) crumbled Maytag blue cheese

1 In small bowl, whisk together all vinaigrette ingredients.

2 In large bowl, toss spinach and basil with half of the vinaigrette. Place on platter. Alternate tomato and onion slices on spinach. Drizzle with remaining vinaigrette. Sprinkle with cheese.

6 servings.

PER SERVING: 220 calories, 18 g total fat (5 g saturated fat), 6.5 g protein, 10.5 g carbohydrate, 15 mg cholesterol, 505 mg sodium, 3 g fiber.